HISTORY & THE POET

Robert Wood has an interest in place, theory and identity. He holds degrees from University of Western Australia, Australian National University and University of Pennsylvania, and has presented lectures at Peking University, Mumbai University and Berkeley University. Wood has edited for *Overland, Peril* and *Cordite,* and worked for Australian Poetry, The School of Life and The Centre for Stories. In 2017–2018, he will be an Endeavour Research Fellow and Visiting Scholar at Columbia University, and a Copyright Agency Emerging Critic with *Sydney Review of Books.*

HISTORY & THE POET

ESSAYS ON AUSTRALIAN POETRY

ROBERT WOOD

Australian Scholarly

First published 2017 by Australian Scholarly Publishing Ltd
7 Lt Lothian St Nth, North Melbourne, VIC 3051
Tel: 03 9329 6963 / Fax: 03 9329 5452
enquiry@scholarly.info / www.scholarly.info
ISBN 978-1-925588-57-6

Cover design: Wayne Saunders
Cover: Sydney 6 am. 23 September 2009

History is the watch the dead keep.

Poetry | a bridge.

For Therese van de Wiele

Contents

Introduction

What is Australia? What is poetry? What is poetry in Australia? These are the basic questions that I asked myself when I wrote *History & the Poet.* Although the nationalist moment has well and truly passed, one is able to see in today's poetics certain fault lines and tendencies of previous decades. There are re-articulations of the repressed that bear thinking about. Indeed, our collective failure to adequately historicise means there is a repetitious quality to much contemporary discourse. For example, Clement Semmler's argument from 1967's *Twentieth Century Australian Literary Criticism* still holds for the most part:

> I mean by 'Australian literary criticism',
> criticism of Australian literature by Australian-
> born scholars and writers, or those writing in
> Australia.*

And the comparative transnational framework Grahame Johnston highlighted in 1962's *Australian Literary Criticism* resonates today:

> We should have a body of work which
> is obviously different in certain of its
> preconceptions and tendencies from the best
> English work over a comparable period, and
> even from the best Canadian or South African or

* For all references please see the back of the book.

New Zealand work.

Finally, Vincent Buckley in 1957's *Essays in Poetry: Mainly Australian* offered something noteworthy when he wrote the following:

> I believe in our poetry; but I also believe that its development is being thwarted by influences within our literary tradition as well as by influences outside it, in society as a whole.

The crucial question might be: what is 'ours'? And with that, who might 'thwart' it? And how has Australian poetry changed since this moment? What I mean to map out with these quotes and questions is the sense that in claiming to 'make it new', I may fall into a paradoxical oldness, that I may simply be stale rather than clearing the air for us to think through where we are now. To that extent, I agree more with Philip Mead when he wrote in *Networked Language* that 'the discourse on poetry in Australia has found it difficult to move beyond a formalist, basically New Critical, paradigm with its origins in the 1940s, a narrowly delimited object of study' rather than when he states, 'there is no longer any disciplinary predominant way.' *History & the Poet* continues to break that paradigmatic origin from the 1940s, to break the definition of literary criticism, comparative transnationalism and the role of influence, through returning to its questions, scanning its archive, speaking back to its empirical style. It contributes to our discussion about Australia as a 'colony', a 'settler society', an 'immigrant nation' while moving suburbanism, the republic and the continent towards the centre.

If the state, poetry and the state of poetry are not what

they used to be, nor are they quite how we think they are. Poetics in Australia now, and at least since Paul Kane's *Australian Poetry: Romanticism and negativity,* is a mutually reinforcing double destabilisation. In its complex dialectical manifestations, one sees that the absence is often an Australian sized one even as there is remarkable resilience in discourses that define 'Australia' as a place with barbed wire boundaries and steel-fenced poetics. Although Clive James might be right when he writes in *Latest Readings* that 'Australian poets don't have to waste their time thinking on nationalist lines at all, because the world is their oyster', to think through, of, against Australia enables our corner of the world to become a little better, a little more pearl than shell in the oyster that is the world. As part of that, we need to re-write Australian poetics through attacking resilient myths of colonialist belonging just as Michael Farrell has done in *Writing Australian Unsettlement.* He has already taken that step for us, so what comes next? What is the utopia that is possible with, in, for *all* people on this continent and those who think of it given our various languages, ideas, bodies?

To my mind, we need to dream once again about what is possible immanently and when we act collectively as citizens. Secondly, the poetry that is analysed is still 'page' poetry presented in a handful of books and journals, which we need to enlarge beyond an English verse tradition and Western orientation. And third, by Australian poetry many still mean poems by those whose identity is 'Australian' as if that was uncontested or not yet complicated by belonging to Othered and multiple locales. This needs to change.

There are, of course, exceptions in the culture at large and in our specific discourse – the Greens' opposition to the Labor-Coalition idea of territorial 'sovereign borders' and the offshore processing of refugees; John Kinsella and Alvin

Pang's *Over There: Poems from Singapore and Australia* with its post-national commitments; the presence of diasporas all over Australia and an increasing engagement with our region that extends Gough Whitlam's foreign policy legacy; Stuart Cooke's comparative lens in *Speaking the Earth's Languages* that asks what comes from juxtaposing settler states from a nomadic perspective; the Yidinji Government that claims legal ownership over territory in Queensland and has citizens who have rejected 'Australia' as a legal and financial entity; and Anita Heiss and Peter Minter's *Anthology of Aboriginal Literature* with its proliferative hopes grounded in country. This might be a type of dialectics worth attending to as a way to undo assumptions and renew what is possible in the here and now. That means we do not need to rescue dead white men such as Semmler, Johnston and Buckley in an unquestioning history but together we can make a philosophical archive of poetic work that has space for the possibilities that are already present within us. Australia, poetry, poetry in Australia can be a refuge for the sick of the sick, the poor of the poor, the mass of the mass, the weak of the weak, the suffering of the suffering. And it is our responsibility and privilege to make that happen.

History & the Poet is part of this hopeful project and it touches on many discourses. This book is in conversation with the metropolitan avant-garde speaking from where I grew up between Redgate and Wembley. This book is in conversation with middle class, liberal, identity politics and how it can limit and distort opportunities for the marginalised as told from a perspective that believes in a coalition of all peoples. This book is in conversation with instrumentalised transatlantic theorising that neglects a common sense philosophy because I like thinking for my self in new keywords. Phrases, words, sensibilities from many places have entered my lingo and for that I am thankful. Yet, this book is also an attempt to localise Australian poetics that uses family *mabarn* as compost. From this, there are peculiar language rituals that express a happy consciousness, precisely because I love crafting songs of my self. And there is a deep and abiding desire for utopia grounded in solidarity. The reader will, of course, find other ways to look at *History & the Poet* and I welcome those interpretations, discussions and possibilities.

I hope that you turn these pages in a warm, salty fire-bath as the sun goes down or after finding the last seat on a peak hour bus in a city filled to the guts or maybe even standing on your head in a t-shirt that says, 'HEALING COUNTRY'. Wherever you read it, I am grateful for your engagement and this opportunity to continue a dialogue we didn't even know we were having towards a way in the world that must keep blossoming.

1

Dear Nephew | Being *Julajulara*

Gamburda, my boy,

It is your birthday and I am away. Maybe you ask where I am. Maybe you cannot say my name. Maybe you ask what is the spirit of the earth that we now share.

Let me tell you that we are not saddened Spain, with their *duende,* which every art and every country is capable of. We say we do not need your *duende* here anyway. We do not need this map or discipline. We do not need that marble and salt, those dark sounds, the roots that cling to the mire that we all know, that we all ignore. We do not need you *duende,* but you are welcome here if you find your way. We have our own possibility of death, our own struggle with dreaming, our own magic that never repeats itself any more than the waves of the sea in a storm.

We are not ancient Hindustan either, with their *thaherao,* that stop and pause they have when they listen, that sitting and waiting and watching for a break in the traffic, that depth of silence. We do not need their good timing, their slowing down, their poise reflecting like gold on anklets that chime when they're dancing. This is their break in the day, their unhurriedness watching the world go by. We can join with them and they can see us, but we do not need their *thaherao* unless we ask them to offer it up.

Yet, we are not civilised England, with their *nostalgia*, that consciousness of barbarism overcome, the light that contains within it a shadow, and casts it so. We are not longing for social contracts or school days proud of starch and long in tooth. We do not miss afternoon scones, tea for two. We are not mindless chatter about the weather in lieu of empire's setting sun. We have not slumbered in such a way that we need to awaken, as if from a dark age whose end we are not sure came anyway, and nor have we risen only to fall into a haze of past glories.

No, dear nephew, we go our own way.

We have our *julajulara*, you and I. That is from your father's country, that country he shares with you. He showed it to me, and *gawarli* was there too. It is your home with birds and beetles and springs and song, and we walked and swam, and he found *tarruru*, that last evening glow above the horizon, that dying down, that peace of mind. He has that, your daddy does. You have it too. You are like him even when you do not know it or cannot show it, not yet but it will come. It is in your name.

We have our *julajulara*, you and I, that washed out cloud, that close to tears, that sadness of life and death. We need that *julajulara* because all night we dance. I cannot sing, I cannot, but dance.

There is no nation and world, no philosophy and poetry, no you and me. There is only *julajulara*, the seed that sits inside.

With this, train yourself for all, learn to haunt with calm, in cloud or groundswell or honeycomb, make yourself a hunter, of death, long for will, never be short of number two, save your nine lives for native cats and one wife, be the best man in the room, strike, work harder than the rest, give in, reset, stop stalk and parry, come back and dance, with me. Then together we can see that *julajulara* is our country, our vision and our feeling.

Now brush your teeth and say, 'Goodnight Moon'.

Love,
Your Uncle Robs

2

Everyday Poetry

As sure as you are reading this now, you will realise that language is all around us. If every word spoken, read, texted, heard and written on a single day in Australia were a drop of water we would find ourselves in a pool deeper than the Mariana Trench. How are we to swim? How should we make our way in this vast ocean of language?

Poetry offers us the ability to splash, frolic and dive. Poetry should not simply be thought of as good prose with line breaks, rhymes with beautiful images or learned sayings about roses. Conservative and avant-garde poets agree that poetry is essentially *metaphoric*. Poetry is about approaching a place but never arriving, suggesting but not saying, showing but not telling. For example, when someone writes 'she drowned in a sea of grief' we could understand that there were a great many tears, but it does not follow that there are so many that she literally drowns in them. There might be other fish to fry, or we might simply have had a whale of a day.

Metaphors are, as Jose Saramago said, 'the best way of explaining things'. They allow us to come at problems from a new angle, to see things with fresh eyes, to apprehend the difficult in a way that is essential. Poetry, as that which trades in metaphors, help us improve our ability to read and write about life differently. It is not only good in and of itself but as training too. Poetry is used to express our selves and communicate with others as well as stop gangs and improve health.

The idea that we face a barrage of language, and that poetry offers us respite from the toughness of life, is not a new one and we can see this in literary criticism about the pastoral poem. The pastoral poem was written by a whole host of Ancients from Hesiod to Theocritus. However, it has taken on an added urgency since the Industrial Revolution and finds renewed expression in our climate-changed era. For literary critic Frank Kermode, the pastoral occurs because of the rise of the modern metropolis – it is the urban idea of a bucolic, untouched paradise. It relies on the city to be produced and captures a different world. In other words, Minerva's owl flies at dusk, meaning that we come to knowledge only after the fact, that we reflect on our nature, our holiday, our Great Barrier Reef only when we begin to lose the thing itself.

If one is so inclined one may write an elegy for, or a love letter to, the sea because we are homesick for it. We know that the Pacific Trash Vortex is not how the ocean is meant to be. The form and style this takes is key. After William Blake's *Songs of Innocence* you might compose a brief rhyming couplet. After Gertrude Stein's *Tender Buttons* you might compose an abstract piece. The question becomes what is the use of the poetic form? Do we seek refuge from modern life in our poems, a therapy that is against the fragmented, overworked condition of our daily grind? Or, do we use poetry to highlight such a life, to go deeper into our alienation, to find, in the surface and play of language, a representation that is as stressed and broken as we are? Do we, in other words, take tourist photo snapshots that make things 'real' or do we paint Picasso style portraits where life is askew?

We can of course do both, and that is why we should swim in the salty waters of confessional, lyric poetry and bathe in the fresh creeks of difficulty and experimentation. This holds for reading other poems and writing poetry in a suburban nation even as we must find oldness anew.

Poetry, in all its fecund and infinite variety, offers so much to living a good life. It nourishes us, awakens, soothes, opens us out to the world in an incomparable way. It can anchor you when you feel like the tide is carrying you out too far, it can float you when you are drowning, it can slake your thirst when you are dry. That is why we need poetry like water every single day of our lives even if it is only in the form of a hello that is also goodbye.

3

History & the Poet

The Poet said, 'Bring out your dead.'

And the poet turned to him and said, 'We do not have any.'

The Poet walked away leaving no trace.

*

The Poet said, 'Bring out your dead.'

I turned to him and asked, 'Who are my dead? I am from ghost country. We are all dead.'

He said, 'You will see them when you bring them.'

And so, I went looking.

*

In the book *Musical Curiosities* from 1811, there is an untranslated song from Bennelong and Yemmerrawanne. It reads:

Barrabula barra ma
mangine wey enguna

This score, which had been sung for an aristocratic

audience in England in 1792, puts love, exchange, music at the root of our history, even as there is an idea, common as air, that Australia has no History of which to speak, and even if it does, that this is new. This is not to isolate our nation however; even Hegel speaks of New Holland as part of the New World, which ties us to the Americas long before Douglas McArthur was stationed here in World War Two. It is, however, to compare Australia in both substance and type to something older, which, in the realm of History, is Europe. What are the effects of this misapprehension? There is, for one, a sense of distant parentage, which is to say a fetish for masters, and the belief in irrevocable origin, which is to say a false consciousness of arrival. That these two linger is incontestable, but how does this congealment of history matter for poetry now?

Paradoxically, where one sees an anti-colonial impetus is in those who perceive that Australia is indeed its own vernacular republic, who rise to the task of refusal precisely because the Federation, founded as it was in 1901, is no longer a collection of colonies even if it is yet to be independent. For them, Australia is capable of producing genius, the latter being a notion many abhor without thought to its fruitful reclamation, critical reinterpretation and contested revelation. That many of today's 'nationalists' do not know how to think through genius means that there is desire for World Historical Men in their material not in their spirit, such that the concept of genius and its poetry remains unchallenged. Hence, the elevation of Les Murray *and his politics* grounded in an anti-modern nostalgia rather than a particular apprehension of the concrete nation from its outbacks to its cities to its frontiers to its archipelagos of islands to its regionalisms and, most normatively, to its suburbs, which, with their straight and regular streets and uniform houses, surround the maze that is the old.

What is the poet in Australia to do?

He must find his own dead, for that will give him his own voice and his own method of madness. He must find his death magic, his *mabarn,* his spirit as an individual power that courses from the soles of his feet to his throat and tongue. He must learn the rituals of the land as it gives language to his society, for that is the province of gods not masters. That is the homegrown permaculture garden where family trees are myths not birthplaces of the sublime or the ridiculous. He must learn how to make it rain in words.

In a 1947 article 'Wuradjeri [*sic*] Magic and Clever Men' Ronald Berndt says the reason we need rain magic is because:

> Eaglehawk those two had a quarrel Turkey those two. After he had gone out for gum, and when he came back he went down to the swamp. When he got there he couldn't find any water; the Eaglehawk when they were all away filled up filled them up he got it all quickly. When he had them all filled the water bags he went up to the place beyond the sky.

Beyond the sky, we know that thunderclouds don't bring rain. Rains come because of poems. Poems come because of rains. Lighting is that death magic, that dance for *mabarn*. In Australia we have the idea that the continent is dry, but that is because we have not been looking at it quite right. *Mabarn* helps you look right, *mabarn* lights it up because it has a cord to the sky and a cord to the dead. And what is history if not the timing the dead keep?

Our history is a universal history. There is suffering, there is love, and there is the love of suffering, and the suffering that comes from love. There are strong spirits we can see if we choose to see them but how we find them in our language depends on what we ask them to do. Will you dance with me? Can I *warni* with you?

In her 1984 poem, 'A Visit to Sun Yat Sen Memorial' Oodgeroo Noonuccal writes:

> *The hall is packed*
> *And I am in my element.*
> *The spirits of the past*
> *Are applauding my efforts.*

But it is us who should applaud her; it is us who should see the dead for being the ground on which the rain that quenches us falls, where we dance. That is history's element.

*

I returned and said, 'I have brought them.'

The Poet looked and said, 'Come now, let us walk, we have places to go and work to do.'

4

Towards History in Australian Poetry

Post-nationalist belonging relies on the maintenance of the nation, albeit rendered as a past. Just as anti-nationalists need a nation to negate, push against, refuse, the post-national needs Australia, if not as a dominant hegemonic force, an agreed upon definition imagined as community, then as an in-situ host of an archipelago. There are no islands without sea. How small those islands are, how big that sea, depends on the frame of looking and representing. I might say that I am mine alone, locate my landedness in the flesh that is my body, and use that as a guide. From this, I know I arrived in Noongar country but that the bodies before me, the bodies that made mine came from India and Scotland or in a different language game Anjengo and Paxton. The designation is 'saltwater' as far back as we know.

What of the poetry that is located in the body? What of poetry that I feel to be mine? This is as much to do with Australians as it is to do with the forebears from my long ago home places. To quarantine poetry in Australia has never been practicable; and, for poetry that claims its derivation elsewhere, one need not minimise the contributions that sit in the archive here. To unpack their complex interaction is a task for historians of the present. In the debates of 'realism' and 'modernism', 'experimentalism' and 'lyric', 'bush ballads' and 'free verse' one glimpses false binaries that offer heuristic comfort but little else. By contrast, reading the archive might enable a renewed sense of pleasure as well as an appeal to the future audience many secretly hope for. There is, after all, interesting writing in our past from Fidelia S.T. Hill to Wolfe Seymour Fairbridge.

But history alone is not enough, which is not an argument for an instrumentalised past reason. It is to suggest that our frames are almost always already backwards looking precisely because the modes of production and contexts of consumption determine a relationship to time that is not linear nor present and advantageous. That is why the failure to question what it means to historicise is problematic.

'Historicising' in my deployment partly refers to how we 'read' texts, which is to say, it is a critique of the simple close reading of a poem. Close reading has its place, but one need attend to other sources in a complex milieu if one is to adequately understand the frame of reference, the symbolic attachments, the literary economy in which particular poems circulate. This is something Martin Duwell moves us towards in the space of reviews. But, we can take it further still. For example, reading the newspaper in 1951 changes how one reads Rex Ingamells' *Great South Land*. In the paper one can find reviews and comments that suggest a complex understanding of the book itself and also reveal the micro-politics and friendships that so matter for coterie and network. Consider, for example, the following review by Ian Mudie in Adelaide's the *Advertiser* from 14 July:

> Many faults will be discovered in the poem:
> inaccuracies, perhaps (but to discover them
> would be cavilling, not criticising); tedious
> passages; limitations of the personal emphasis;

> the failure to touch sublimity; the acceptance of a scale of values rather rhapsodical than creative; the lack of critical pruning; a certain monotonous regularity in the verse; the prevalence of a spirit of doggedness, often where one would rather have inspiration; the inclusion of much material which some may think irrelevant and unprogressive; the sense, overruling all, that Mr. Ingamells is a poet of pedestrian rather than Olympian gifts. All this, or much of it, is true. But there is an unanswerable retort: the book has weight; it is convincing in spite of these objections.

My immediate reaction is that this review pulls few punches, something that cannot be said for today's featherbed standard. This review informs our idea of Ingamells and *Great South Land* because of its textual nuance and historical depth. One might say, this is simply New Historicism, but my response would be that it participates in a language game based on specific source material that does not unrealistically silo a poem. In other words, it has a reality quotient that provides a more complex interpretation, one that might be charming because of its very gesture towards attentiveness.

If one were so inclined one could also find that Mudie and Ingamells had previously been correspondents before a breakdown in communication, some sort of spat between them that changes the public discourse. It not only implies that aesthetic judgements do not occur in a vacuum, but also that specific social relations manifest with very real criticisms in print more generally.

History, of a cultural, economic, social or political iteration, is a necessary if somewhat unquestioned part of literary conversations now. Uncovering those frames means not only renewing historical poetics, but relying on skills that many take for granted. That is to say, philosophical interrogation and contextual synthesising need complement close reading as an assumed part of method. *What* one reads is incredibly important. Poetics depends on the sources that determine the world outside the poetry. The mid-century of Ingamells, for example, was beset by beliefs in the 'dying race' something that manifested most explicitly in child removal discourses including those of government policy. It comes through too in the Jindyworobak displacement of Indigenous bodies as real, living people. This is one aspect of *Great South Land* that is noteworthy now. But people today speak of 'closing the gap', 'social inclusion', 'recognition' and 'treaty' with very little precedence, or attention to these as historically contingent discourses, preferring to gloss them as new. Often, we are stuck in paradigmatic ways of thought without recourse to genuine freedom.

Indeed, if one reads poetry and criticism from the immediate post-war era in Australia one is struck by how similar many terms of the debate are to those today. Work by Ingamells, Ted Strehlow, Roland Robinson, Nancy Cato and Judith Wright all grapple with eco-poetics, settlement and Indigeneity in ways that are salutary now. But so too did their putative 'opposition', A.D. Hope and Douglas Stewart, who offer a way of reading these issues precisely because of their noteworthy absence. In general one could characterise the period from 1946 to 1968 as being one of 'nationalists' and 'Anglophiles'; the former taking as their content Australian matters, particularly an appropriated Aboriginalia with a left liberal political frame; the latter taking as their content seemingly universal, though British inflected, tropes of love, war, nature. Both of them, however, are concerned with voice, albeit not always lyric, in such a way that offers more lessons for today.

History offers one avenue towards a different territory precisely because it does not claim to find an origin point, but merely enables us to attend to the ethics and aesthetics we find important and influential. We do not need to re-invent the wheel but perfect the axle. If one goes back far enough one realises that there are no answers but simply more questions, and asking them will help our writing and our lives as they continue to unfold.

That we *can* do this means we need more historical scholarship. The field of Australian history indicates there is the strong possibility for developing a locally important and centrally influential way of reading the archive. That history and criticism should so often be in service to poetry, simply yoked to it through a post-doctoral course of study, leaves an emaciated body poetic that fails to serve the muse well enough. Poets need critics, and critics need history, which is a synthetic activity of theorising, research and ethics. History as a necessary endeavour brings to consciousness aspects of the aesthetic that are philosophical.

We can, of course, believe in the possibility of being Australian again, which *seems* like an anachronistic position. But it might simply be its own negation. Our tradition is the whole of culture, which necessarily means sharpening our poetics without superstition and in a materialist way that unpacks the economies of how it comes to be important in the first place. The importance of that belongs as much to the past as it does to the present and future, to the poet, historian and philosopher all bailing water together in a ship that wants to sink but is better off sailing to safe shores.

5

The Poetics of Daily Life

When we think about our daily lives we may begin to think about what is familiar to us. We do not think about the whiskey in heaven or the fire in hell. We think of routine – of waking up in the morning, wiping the sleep from our eyes, standing in the shower letting the water run over us. We eat breakfast on autopilot and only begin to come alive when we stumble outside to grab a coffee. Or perhaps we are morning people – we are inspired by the light streaming into our room, jump out of bed and greet the day with a sun salutation, ride our bike to work and smile at our colleagues who are clutching those coffees as if they were life-buoys in an altogether unforgiving sea of paper, technology, meetings, obligations and familiarity.

Regardless of how we start the day, it proceeds in a similar way for all of us. We work, we eat, we go through the motions before we get home to books, dinner, TV or maybe go out to the movies with friends or visit a bar or gallery. When we think of daily life we do not think of life altering events. The rhythm of Monday to Friday demands that it be repetitious and normal. If every day was overwhelming we simply could not cope, or, we would find a new equilibrium and quickly redefine what familiar is to us.

By contrast, we encounter poetry at important rituals.

There may be a playful, mocking limerick at a 21st birthday party; a heartfelt, sentimental sonnet at a wedding; or, perhaps, an elegiac lament at a funeral. For most of us, poetry is not an every day encounter and while we may remember that someone said something that rhymed to celebrate a particular moment in time, it is for the most part a marginal cultural artefact. When we think about poetry we might think of it as language that is unfamiliar, or 'defamiliarised'. Viktor Shklovsky introduced the term 'defamiliarised' in his 1925 essay 'Art as Technique' and used it as a way to differentiate 'habit' from art. We could think of habit as automatic, assumed, naturalised, entrained. In other words habit is about the everyday, it is the sleep we wipe from our eyes, the route we take to work on our bike, the coffee we order regularly. We have become so used to this way of living, this way of engaging with the world and language, that it is all but unconscious.

In contrast poetry 'exists that one may recover the *sensation* of life; it exists to make one feel things, to make the stone stony'. Poetry makes one aware of the perception of things, which could mean becoming aware of the difficulty of language, the constructedness of language, the fact that there are multiple meanings and strange arrangements of words all around us. We know poetry is to some degree a performance of language. It is like a stone in the shoe that makes you aware of every step.

Poetry, especially that which takes us out of our habits, is important because it makes perception less automatic. When we think poetically we think out of our comfort zone. As an analogy when we look at the painted walls of our home we do not see a canvas by Mark Rothko. But both a Rothko and a poem can function as relief from the everyday. They potentially allow us to look at walls and words anew.

And so, poetry can function as a holiday from the normal way we interact with language. And if we think of our holidays we can think of all the different types of places we have been and the experiences we have had. It could be a bacchanalian revelry with friends at a beachside villa in Bali; it could be an educational tour of ruins in Italy; it could be a quick weekend getaway to the coast where we do nothing but read the papers, go out for breakfast and take a walk along Wilson's Promontory. This fits with Terry Eagleton's definition of the literary. As Eagleton states in *How to Read a Poem*:

> Literature transforms and intensifies ordinary language, deviates systematically from everyday speech. If you approach me at a bus stop and murmur "Thou still unravished bride of quietness," then I am instantly aware that I am in the presence of the literary.

If you try this line of verse at a bus stop, not only will people be aware that they are in the presence of the poetic, they will also be aware they are in the presence of someone a little bit mad. But the idea that poets are a little bit mad goes back at least as far as Horace and, perhaps at this bus stop, they could be forgiven because we all need a little bit of madness to get through the day.

Poetry forces us to reflect precisely because it is uncommon. Having read this, you might be thinking 'That is all very well, I get that poetry is something different from saying hello to my barista, but what if I have read from Sappho to Stein?' If you read these poets' works like they are the newspaper, maybe poetry is your daily life. Yet, in a sense, all of us are always translating from one language to another – the IT department speaks a very different English to the marketing manager. Or, to return and extend our earlier metaphor, our downtime during the everyday could be thought of as a micro-holiday. The coffee might not be a massage at sunset in an exotic location but it functions as therapy in a similar way. From this we get a broad idea of what poetry is and it is also apparent that one cannot quite ask for a coffee without articulating what kind of coffee one wants, not the metaphor that best describes the drinking experience.

Poetry is not just the things we recognise as poetry, the great lines from Ovid to T.S. Eliot. It could be thought of as noticeable asides even in everyday contexts. Poetics as the study of poetry recognises this. It takes place when we say something like 'did you notice what she said in that meeting?' Language in this case is recognisable, as a surface, as a network, as a system of signs, not as a natural empty vehicle for expression. We begin to think about the quality of words themselves not only what they are saying and what they refer to. And that is thinking poetically.

But what is the poet to do? What if you are an elite sportsperson whose second home is the MCG? What if your everyday is someone else's holiday? What is the poet's poetry?

Firstly, we might say that the archive is inexhaustible. A poet could get lost trying to read the corpus of poetry in Australia and that is only a small part of the world's library. Some people dedicate their entire careers to one individual's poems. For example, whole groups of people gather to traipse through the Lake District and read William Wordsworth each year. There are scholars who only study Emily Dickinson. There is a certain consolation in this, in knowing that there is a wealth of poetry from the past, precisely because we all know that the past is another country. Poetry's past is a perfect place for a holiday even for a poet whose everyday is different to yours and mine.

But in thinking about a poetics of the everyday we might think of how poetry enters into our lives as a certain type of language. If pulp fiction is the blockbuster movie of the world, literary fiction is the festival film equivalent. And poetry is the homemade recording of a performance art piece. It is obscure but recognising that gives poetry a certain power. There are very few barriers to entry. After all, it is the research and development wing of language, the place for experimentation and extremity and we can be invited in to play and dabble with relative freedom.

The intention to re-frame our daily language as poetry is much the same as how Marcel Duchamp liberated a urinal from its surrounds, put it in a gallery and called it art. For most of us here, Duchamp represents a certain type of holiday – one where we eat $1 hot dogs, visit MOMA, buy an 'I Love New York' t-shirt, take in a show on Broadway and get lost catching the A-train back to JFK. But our lives, the lives we share right here and now, have a different cadence, a different sensibility, a different aim. For a poetry of the everyday on this land mass, we might want to imagine a vast collective endeavour that meant we could holiday in our own place, that meant we could travel without the customs hassle, the cost of insurance or the embarrassment of speaking in a foreign tongue as if we were children or imbeciles. That might mean we simply intentionalise our language as a way to get out of our habits. And we can do this while acknowledging that we need the local forms that poetry takes be that readings, book launches or poetry classes.

After all, it is remarkably easy to include poetry in one's daily life, to make this linguistic ritual as simple as a prayer before dinner. For every episode of 'This American Life' there is a poetry podcast online; for every cat video there is a poem in the digital Australian Poetry Library; and instead of CandyCrush there is a poetry app that gives you a poem for the day. Indeed, for every drop of rain there is a word waiting to be turned into a message in a bottle simply by using your mind poetically.

Everyone can write poetry. Everyone can reframe the language that is around them to be poetic. Everyone can approach the words that dictate how we think about our daily life. The key might be whether or not we can make that compelling for an audience, whether we can make it good poetry, whether we can cut a David from the rough stone found in a quarry that is our daily life. And that is where reading and craft matters. To be a good poet one needs to read poetically and that means looking at the world a certain way. It also means reading the archive and one's contemporaries on a daily basis as if it were breakfast, a ride to work or a coffee. Poetry needs an audience as much as we need poetry. If we think that poetry is all around us we can look at the world a little differently and travel without ever leaving home. That is what poets can do for the daily life of all of us in the here and now.

6

In the Pacific Theatre

As a society we like the shiny new gadget, the fifteen-minute fame of the reality celebrity, and the latest food craze. The creative destruction inherent in this, and the presence of inbuilt obsolescence, would suggest that we suffer from a myth of invention. Poets suffer from this myth too, but, in so many ways, our present moment echoes the global moment of the 1940s and 50s. That I choose to see this era as a starting point is due as much to the birth of my parents as it is to the birth of suburbia and the contours of today's world in aesthetic and political terms. That this was also the global high-water for socialist realism means we must think through Dorothy Hewett, the 1946 Pilbara Strike, the USSR, the Pink Decade and of course their negations.

Socialist realism as an aesthetic movement emanated directly from the iron hand of Joseph Stalin. Established in 1933, it sought to create art that was:

> Proletarian: relevant to the workers and understandable to them.
>
> Typical: scenes of everyday life of the people.
> Realistic: in the representational sense.

Partisan: supportive of the aims of the State and the Party.

Socialist realism spread with the soft power reaches of the USSR's 'engineers of the soul'. In the early years of the Cold War it had a stronghold in Australia with many poets adopting these principles in their writing practice while also being active members of the Communist Party. There were, of course, negotiations to this, and they were not the only political actors from literature and the arts more generally. The other groups included nationalists (Ingamells), constitutional monarchists (Douglas Stewart), right wing sympathisers (Ian Mudie), and leftist modernists (the later Hewett). To the latter group, the politicisation of art not only meant the creation of statist propaganda but the radicalism of form, which is not quite the same as arguing for *art pour l'art*.

Indeed, it is arguable that the first mode of realism, that of the late nineteenth century, was a greater political intervention than socialist realism precisely because it shifted the paradigm of perception and the language of expression. Given that perception is what language enables, and what ideological state apparatuses trade in, and reflecting on the fact that power is everywhere so much so that the base interacts with the superstructure, an aestheticisation of aesthetics might be more political for writers than determining what Communism or Fascism are in truth and effect. We are, after all, superbasic.

The American scene was similarly engaged in a culture battle, to which one need only reference the Ford Foundation and the Congress for Cultural Freedom. You cannot, after all, have a war with only one side. 'Capitalism', thought of here in very simple terms as the marketing, incorporation and distribution of liberal subcultures that were not state based, becomes a hallmark of post-war America and includes the conquest of cool and the rise of the youth market in the 1960s. Rebellion was commodified with Beat poets, hippies, and Ben & Jerry's. This not only implies we need to attend to how poets become celebrities but how power always relies on remaking itself anew.

To me, the limits of language are the limits of the world, and the Communist state sought to limit not only discourse, but the entire system of signs through a centralist radiation. That America, its putative opposition, fed its citizens a steady diet of limitless freedom is hardly comfort enough, but in the Australian archive one notices that both sides of the Cold War sold dreams and nightmares in a language that is as different and similar to ours as we can imagine. That they relied on each other, that they enjoyed the fight because it gave them reason for critique, meant that self-realisation was mediated through a bogeyman Other. As long as there was an 'ism' to fight they could not complain at all.

What that might mean for realism today is the thinking through of our reality effects – how does social media disrupt *and* reinforce patterns of behaviour not only from holiday rentals to taxis but also literary networks and poetry? How does climate change correlate to the Bomb as an existential shadow? How does the rise of China as a hybrid of the Cold War augur well or bode ill for our place in the world be that through the uptake of Ezra Pound's Mandarin ideograms or the reception of J.H. Prynne in Beijing?

When Australian poets express their wish that our leaders read poetry, like Barack Obama reads Claudia Rankine, we might need to be careful wishing for our enmeshment with systems of power that are not adequately our own. *Citizen,* no matter its virtue, does not stop the drones in Syria or the floods in Oklahoma and it is a sobering reminder to realise that for all the politics of socialist realists they were unable to stop the gulags or colonisation of nature that the Soviets have since become known for.

7

Please Form an Orderly Line

Please answer the following question:

a) uncritical importation of metropolitan theorist
b) repetitive citation of academic field
c) selective close reading of poetic text
d) journalistic prose with emphasis on clarity
e) affirmation to solve a problem
f) all of the above

If you selected (f) your essay is now complete.

The Australian poetics essay (verbal and written) in Australia often remains untroubled by formal distinction. Still, I love the common essay form including Katie Hansord's unironic commentary in 'The Literary Dawn'; the mocking assemblage of Michael Farrell's 'Kangaroo and Lyrebird'; and the straight sentimentalism of Toby Davidson in 'Francis Webb and the 1960s'. That all of them reach for a non-establishment poetry (feminist, transnational, insane respectively) and tell their story in a linear fashion would suggest a separation of form from content. But their separation is not the same as explicating the dialectic, which is to say that in our language games form *is* separate from content. The easy poem can have a difficult poetics just as the difficult poem can have an accessible poetics, just as simple subject matter can have complex syntax or any other such interrelationship between the constitutive parts of poetics as sociology, aesthetics and ethics.

There are, of course, attempts to play with the standard, from Ali Cobby Eckermann's vernacular 'Give Me Back My Mother's Heart' to Stuart Cooke's estranged 'Australian Bricolage' to *The Lifted Brow*'s Experimental Non-Fiction Prize. There would seem to be, however, a systemic failure of dialectical essays precisely because the nation has concretised what is normative in a way that sits awkwardly with its truth content. Oddly enough, it falls to Clive James to make clear how the category 'Australia' connects with the avant-garde when he writes in 'The Great Generation of Australian Poetry':

> In theory there *was* no literary life, but in practice a supposedly philistine society was already saturated with poetry at many layers ... viewed on the Australian scale, there is something to what [Peter Porter] says that Sydney University is a hot spot. The thing to bear in mind is that in the 1940s it wasn't that yet. The upcoming literary mandarins would help to make it so, but at the time *they were not joining a new power structure.*

According to James, what we find in the network most associated with Australia's nationalist poetry is a key quality of the avant-garde, namely its pre-emptive temporality. One might be tempted to dismiss this as a function of youth, but that disregards the influential sense of timing that matters for critical reflection now. One can discover avant-garde nationalists, but the point is not that there are local experimental scenes. It is that this critical understanding of Australia shares a self-defining characteristic with the vanguard of post-modernism. This is not to argue that Peter Porter et al were up to what Charles Olson et al were up to but that in our history we might benefit from their juxtaposition. If one wanted to make a claim of Australia's delayed arrival, one would first need to find out what arriving meant and what being out of time was as well. Re-orienting our canons might stop them firing.

That the spirit of the avant-garde can be found in the national persuasion is not enough to combine the two, to chart the middle way by being all-inclusive. This means that there is no Australian avant-garde, no avant-garde Australia in the hybrid sense of definition. We do not need a common ground but a higher one. This is salted caramel not chilli chocolate. A true poetics of the contemporary that is based in a country that exists in the continent mislabelled 'Australia' neither mimics metropolitan inventiveness nor resolves itself to isolated traditions, but doubles this shared futurity without the expectation of its reification through the late arrival of delayed gratification or external validation. This is not an argument against the avant-garde or specialisation lest we simplify Kate Middleton in 'The Future of Poetry' when she writes:

> How often does a lyrical poet turn to, say, Ted Berrigan's *Sonnets* with their repetitive cut-up structures? How often does the experimental poet make a serious study of the lyrical naturalist Mary Oliver? We are natural specialisers, but what I wish we would more

> naturally become is *celebrators* ... Our futures often come about from retracing our steps a little or a long way, and then making a different turn.

In agreeing with Middleton about celebration, I would argue that we are also not specialist enough, for specialisation leads to the universal, and so, after acknowledging that the avant-garde and the Australian are not so dissimilar after all, we might find firm footing in our bodies themselves. In our doubling, we could focus on the past as myth not narrative, expelling the story of Douglas Stewart's *Glencoe,* but leaving behind questions as questions and punctuation as punctuation, which is what we see in Claire Nashar's *Lake.* Yet there can be neither nostalgia for origins as answers or for a specific utopia that never was. Can we mourn remains that we did not know we had? Can we mourn the death of James, which has not come yet, or the avant-garde as it tries to redefine itself? Maybe not even time itself will tell when it arrives in a place that was predicted a long time ago.

8

You Must Let Go of the Anger in May

Said the official verse culture antagonist to the suburbanist:

'Yours is a proscriptive essay – administrative and alienated and angry yet masquerading as balanced. It is not a project for anyone else, but maybe it can generate heat and light as a prose critique of what is happening somewhere in the archive, which is infinite.'

The suburbanist replied:

'Let me repeat: If we take for a moment a wide view of contemporary poetry in Australia we see the resilience of lyric, prose and narrative, which highlight stylistic elements such as clarity, rhyme and feeling. We see this in spoken word and slam, expressions of official culture like Hansard, bush ballads, and the literary bureaucratic establishment more generally, which is itself an international phenomenon. These stylistic qualities are less common in academic poetry and traditionally inflected song poems, but few have pushed poetry to a logical end of words. Pete Spence's visual work might be one such endpoint, but limiting ourselves to language as language we see in many of today's poems a number of techniques that half dissolve narrative prose.

Many live after L=A=N=G=U=A=G=E, but few live as

it. There is no comparable, or adequate, rupture precisely because there is a lack of historical, and philosophical, work being done. Cue the misunderstanding of what to radically break with. This might be because of the paradox of university scholarship now. We live in a moment after the national mythmaking of bygone days in an era informed by the black armband view that is predominant institutionally. This is a good thing, for it means there is no agreed upon history, if ever there appeared to be one. Having no collective understanding of a tradition to push against and a field of inheritance helps account for the common and superficial engagement with the contemporary. This means that the best one can do is simply capture the zeitgeist, sublimating this into a melange that flattens difference, distinction and knowledge. It ends up being anti-intellectual, which is not necessarily an altogether bad thing. But it helps explain the ecosystem. No wonder people trade heavily on personality and become obsessed with an internecine, close-in focus rather than a deep past or a relevant future.

Our history as our experience makes up our poetry, throwing into question the very notion of 'ourness' and realising it is a performative utterance that brings into question what the limits, porosity and boundaries of experience and 'the before' are. This is not to be prescriptive about the type of influences that are 'good' or 'valuable', but to suggest that how we read, how we frame is not yet critical and hence creative enough. Why read L=A=N=G=U=A=G=E when you can read what they read, or read *how* they read? This should not be a way to throw the baby out with the bathwater even if the baby can be an asshole.

Our historical and philosophical work needs to go back far further. We need examine ourselves in the oldest forms of thinking and language that are available to us. This is not to binarise originality and repetition, to place a premium on beginnings instead of genealogies. It might be that our work is not unoriginal or derivative enough, that mimicry can be a politicised strategy for us in today's colony rather than the embarrassment it is held to be going back, of course, to Plato.'

The official verse culture antagonist asked:

'What then is the cure?'

And the suburbanist answered:

'The cure is not necessarily singular; we must have many cures for many ills and it is not to have a project. But it is not not to have a cure and not not to have a project. The originary rupture that I seek in Australian language is as poetic as it is political. It is a radical deformation and a reformed utopianism. There are many ways to enable this. Recontextualisation is one such method. This might occur when we take a settler conceptual poem into a legislative assembly. It might also look like a sound bite, or policy piece, taken into a poetry reading. But this relies on an understanding of context, which can be seen as a type of historical work. Historically, Australia is a colony but the sands are shifting. We need poetry that continues to stand against the language hegemony that emanates from the Queen herself. This happens at the level of content, form and style as well as language in general.

However, no poet working in Australia today has realised the potential of the available linguistic material. That may be impossible, but surely the ambitious search for it need be attempted. Of course, there are dextrous, nimble, thorough, able, adept, charming, intelligent, sensitive, aware, alert, challenging, difficult, admirable poets working today. There is also potentially far more than that. To undo the Australian poetry mind means recognising that the material here, as a type of available truth content, need be re-expressed linguistically. But such is the conformity to structural limitations, the narrowing of available experience and the strength of the paradigmatic mentality that the possibility of new poetry, and with it revolutionary decolonisation, seems distant. In specific terms, the hegemonic use of English, the slim band of influences and the geographic concentration of the literary bureaucratic establishment has meant the limitation of poetic, and hence political, possibility.

Of course, some poets counter the dominance of English. There is a whole host of linguistically diverse Others, which Michelle Cahill discusses in 'Extimate Subjects'. However, there are not enough poets working in Aboriginal Englishes, let alone with traditional Indigenous languages in and of themselves. This is not to dismiss those Englishes, their located content or their idiolectical expression in, say, Marion May Campbell, Sam Wagan Watson, Ken Canning, Philip Hall, Tony Birch, Jeanine Leane, Lee Cataldi or Evelyn Araluen. It is to suggest that traditional linguistic knowledge is under valued in society as a whole. Nowhere is this clearer than in governmental policies toward the teaching of Indigenous languages, which means that it is rare for students, or nascent emerging poets, to encounter those languages in ideological state apparatuses.

Quite simply, where does one go to learn Warlpiri, Noongar, Yolngu or any other such language? Must one go to the country those languages are spoken in? But one need asks: how does one gain permission? Such is the complicated and confusing legacy of new settlement governmentality. But many poets use the present situation simply as an excuse for a lack of genuine engagement and in so doing become complicit, through absence, in the egregious fact of occupation. One can read a whole host of linguistic material in Indigenous languages – there are wordlists, dictionaries and other such sources that retain the original, and there is also the Bible and a host of literary, and poetic, materials that have been translated back and forth in countless languages. That we should continue to be so uneducated on Indigenous matters is plainly criminal.

It goes without saying that there are culturally sensitive documents; but it goes with saying that those are contested, that attempts need be made regardless, that the archive is bountiful and that one can visit country without ever leaving one's computer. If Gerald Murnane can become fluent in Hungarian and never leave the state of Victoria, why shouldn't people know what *julajulara* means? There is a great silence on Indigenous languages in the poetry community, not so much a cult of forgetfulness but a willed dismissal of that which is *actually* difficult. Unless one comes to terms with, plays with, cultivates a relationship with Indigenous language one cannot expect to create a poetry that resonates with the nature and society here. It is the firm bedrock of language reality that exists in Australia. All else is topsoil.

This heavy presence of English contributes to the lack of diversity in reading and influence, which skews American and Western European (often in translation). This comes about in the poets of influence and emerges in names mentioned explicitly in the poetry itself, in the content in other words. This may be as the subject of a whole book or in specific poems. This is not to suggest that locals don't matter, but that influence still comes from on high, which is no one poet's fault. Nowhere is the lack of diversity clearer than in review culture, which might be said to reveal the points of reference in the network if only because that is what reviewers project onto poets, of whom they read in their reading. As Ben Etherington wrote in 'The Poet Tasters':

> The poetic education and tastes of those in the poetry community are structurally Eurocentric. It seems all Australian poets took the same two courses at university: 'British and Irish poetry from Wordsworth to Heaney' and 'Modern American poetry from Whitman to L=A=N=G=U=A=G=E'. A handful also took a course on French symbolism. When Australian poet critics say 'poetry' they mean a particular verse tradition and a sequence of aesthetic developments. Confining ourselves to English-language poetry, you could count on one hand references in all 2013 reviews [which totalled 247] to poets from the Caribbean, South and South-East Asia, African and Pacific nations (including New Zealand). Critic Watch would like to cite examples, but you can't cite an absence.

As Etherington states, it is a structural issue, much like the lack of Indigenous language knowledge in the mainstream poetry ecosystem. The decline of canonical studies seemed pronounced a generation ago, but the rear-guard action, which has taken the form of an ongoing preference for the Eurocentric cited above, means that the poetry being produced today is a poor reflection of the society we live in.

Poets working today need their writing to reflect their local experience. What that looks like depends, of course, on the life lived but one can assume that means interacting with a diversity of cultures. We cannot jettison Europe or America, but if one so easily eats burritos why shouldn't one read Homero Aridjis? To not engage with the linguistic possibilities afforded by diversity means that we fail to understand the world that is already here, let alone the one that is coming closer to us day by day. No wonder the sales figures are small, no wonder many feel as though they are preaching to the converted. We need diversity and not simply through the propagation of a specific identity politik, or outside our most prestigious journals and awards.

This is not aided by the ongoing geographical limitations of poetry influencers. It is naïve to think that Melbourne and Sydney do not dominate poetry today in real terms – publications, festivals, journals, circulation. The volume and strength of publishing houses makes it clear that these two cities are the epicentres. For example, in Melbourne there is Cordite, Whitmore, 5Islands, Black Pepper, Hunter, and Spinifex. In Sydney there is Giramondo, Puncher & Wattman, Grand Parade Poets, and Pitt Street Poetry. Cordite keeps growing and growing, and, Giramondo alone covers an awful lot of poetic territory when it comes to books. Needless to say there are publishers in other places – UQP (Brisbane); Walleah (Hobart); Fremantle and UWA Press (Perth); Ginninderra (Canberra); Brandl & Schlesinger (Blue Mountains), Vagabond (Tokyo).

However, no matter where we are in Australia, one generally sees an urban or rural consciousness in the type of poetry published that sits at odds with the suburban material where so many live. There is, it seems, a fetish for the country voice and the urban affect. But to put it another way, how are we to reflect on the majoritarian existence of people here when our publishing houses are based in a handful of electorates? There are of course, people to counter this, people who write about suburbia from Jill Jones to Lachlan Brown, Fiona Wright, Omar Sakr and Zenobia Frost. And their work, for this alone, should be applauded.

We need to adapt Charles Blackman, Arthur Boyd, David

Boyd, John Brack, Bob Dickerson, John Perceval, Clifton Pugh, Bernard Smith when they wrote in 'The Antipodean Manifesto' in 1959 that:

> We are not, of course, seeking to create
> a national style. But we do seek to draw
> inspiration from our own lives and the lives of
> those around us. Life here in this country has
> similarities to life elsewhere and also significant
> differences. Our experience of this life must be
> our material.

We must see that each life is multiple and individual. Nor am I suggesting there need be a national style even as the state need become allied and activist. Country is decidedly different from nation, and we need express in language of our own making what it means to live as or with Indigenous people from Yamatji to Koori land. That means taking seriously the rich and living heritage of various communities in languages that are Indigenous to them with respect to the traditions that continue to matter. People need experience a wide variety of life – remote communities often need volunteers, which means there are Countries in Australia that await learning from; Australians are free to travel and often do to a great many foreign nations that are not the retiree Contiki array that counts for the reading lists of reviewers; and one is able to pass through the suburbs, even dwell there, without much limitation. Only when poets see that the linguistic expression of these experiences are vital to freedom in the here and now will we begin to see a type of poetry that is worthy of the name.'

And the interlocutor said:

‘That may be so, but it does not matter, you need let the ecosystem flower. We are playing games and another house can be added in any direction. Do not wall off the possibility of multiplicity in what you say. Let go of the anger in May.’

9

Crow and *Kurrugu*

Think for a moment of the 'literary novel' in contemporary Australia, which might mean, Alexis Wright (*Carpentaria*), Kim Scott (*Benang*), John Coetzee (*Childhood of Jesus*), Richard Flanagan (*Narrow Road to the Deep North*), Anna Funder (*All that I Am*), Christos Tsiolkas (*Barracuda*), Alex Miller (*Coal Creek*) and Tim Winton (*Breath*). One might want to compare these to the novel historically – time and tradition (Austen, Dickens) or their intersection with modernism and post-modernism (Sterne, Joyce; Pynchon, Wallace) or the local (Marquez, Achebe) or maybe, even globalisation (Adiche, Keyi) and history itself (Eco, Mantel). But I mean this order based on formal inventiveness, based upon a reified idea of 'the literary', an idea that seems like a rock-bottom even as it would pay to excavate it through a philology, archaeology and genealogy that was not strictly national. What these novels may be said to share is an aspiration towards 'poetry', which is the *ur* of literature or, to put it another way, the literary aspect of the literary novel. This rests on a congealed idea of what poetry is but more importantly our novelists are sure never to meet it. That is to say, it is a commonplace in reviews, in conversation, in criticism, to argue that a novel's literariness depends on its 'poetry'. But, poetry actually means death in the marketplace.

Although 'the average reader' might be able to name Omar Musa or Maxine Beneba Clarke, it is doubtful they will own their books of poetry. This is confirmed by the shelf-space devoted to poetry in bookstores, where it is often confined to an inconspicuous place far away from the window displays that pull in passers by, far away from cooking and design. Poetry is a nuisance to the novel's dominance.

The idea of the novel as dominant market player is based upon the expectation, true to a large degree, that the audience simply wants a good story. This goes some way to explaining its intrinsic power, which has been marketed to the full potential through trailer videos, speaking tours, literary festivals and the corresponding marginalisation of contemporary poetry. One might be tempted to suggest that the market has it wrong, that the abstract versifier is the *true* repository of 'literariness'. Hence, poets can take solace in the dated high culture arguments of bygone days or the fact that one will arrive after one dies. That popular media commentators and writers festivals often promote this type of poetry means that such a view can be made without fear of losing lobster bisque let alone bread and water. That they are critiqued for hypocrisy because they continue to publish, which can be read as a form of selling out (even as it might be best to think of it as buying in), only extends the enmity rather than thinking of the limits of the game in the first place.

Asking how far one can push 'difficulty' today is simply re-applied modernism (Eliot, Dada, Kurt Schwitters, Concrete), and in thinking through the literary, seen here in the novel *and* poem, we might avoid asking what is their hybrid be that the narrative poem (Philip Hall), poetic novel (Christine Evans) or individual author (Musa). We might avoid this especially as the first is 'conservative', the second 'innovative' and the third 'rare' when judged on a political, aesthetic, social axis that revolves around defamiliarisation, which is itself based on an assumed formal context of intelligibility. Instead, we might ask: where have the novel and poem come from and how does this manifest now?

In other words, I want to know what the respective totems of the novel and the poem are. What animal spirits did they evolve from? This is not the same as asking what are their origins and, as is common, privileging the roots of the novel in the epic or *Don Quixote,* and the roots of the poem in the ode and *Eugene Onegin*. Instead, it is my desire to relocate their particular articulation of the universal spirit, which is Natural, in individual animals who were their first narrators albeit in tongues. Of course, today's particular linguistic artefact (this novel, that poem) has its own spirit – Salman Rushdie's *Midnight's Children* might be a tiger and Jerome Rothenberg's *A Seneca Journal* is a beaver – but in speaking of ideal types let's think through heuristics as metaphors.

The novel is a crow, the poem a *kurrugu*.

In a *tabi* called 'The Crows' in Karierra by Tjarndai, he sings:

Njalataianna pannina kudii nagunjuru
Pilanmannaba takanna.
Palakuru pala kardiiriba pannigu
Tinatingala juurra-manjulaba mirrunjgu
Palakuru pala waarnarraba warnjga "kaa"
Warnda murrumurru tanbatirriiba wurdanjga

They lurk and sit till they see a bone
What they can get, they grab
They hang around, eyeing something off.
Hopping about in the sun,

Conversing: "Kaa, kaa, kaa."
Then its up to the back of a branch
One after another – what a crowd.

This is the day-to-day and the lifecycle of the crow who 'lurks' and 'sees a bone'. It is a picture of them as a collective ('they') who are active ('hopping' and 'eyeing'), and most importantly 'being a crowd'. The novelist in today's ecosystem is part of a wider network – they have agents, publicists, editors, publishers. By comparison, the poet seems positively solitary, which is not to say lonely or separate, for poets congregate at readings, conferences, book launches. But poets do so amongst themselves without a bureaucracy or administration. That the publishers, readers and critics of poetry also happen to be poets is evidence of how self-contained a world it truly is.

The poet is a *kurrugu*. From a *tjalurra* in Yindjibarndi by Robert Churnside, we know that:

Ku-urru murlawarnjgaa juurumarna karnalilila
Ku-urru murlawarnjgaa juurumarna tarritogula

Kurrugu bird-call finds his melody in the morning
Kurrugu bird-call finds his melody in the treehole.

The poet does find his melody at the beginning, dawning with the sun, and he finds it in a treehole, the place where the bird makes its home. Given today's diversity, what makes a poem is less the formal qualities of the artefact, and more the framing that would appoint a poet *as a poet* not simply a writer in general.

One may ask what is the higher synthesis of novel and poem. What happens when crow and *kurrugu* mate? This might be about finding the origin of language itself, of saying that the crow comes from ash. The next question is how do ash and the ancestors of *kurrugu* relate? If the synthesis is to be found in a genre, it is to be found in the proverb, which is narrative and metaphor in a higher sense both with accessibility like the pulp novel including crime, science fiction, romance and ideas like the poem as philosophy. This is not to deny its expressive function, but to relocate the potential of language *as sacred ritual* in the face of a market that would hold out very little place for diversity and the absolutely literary in the first place.

10

No Jailbreak but On Parole

In her review of Lionel Fogarty's *Eelahroo (Long Ago) Nyah (Looking) Möbö-Möbö (Future)* Fiona Hile writes:

> In June 2013, Fogarty attended the *apoetic* Festival of Innovative Australian Poetry at the NSW Writing Centre, partly in order to participate in a tribute to the poetry of [Oodgeroo] Noonuccal and [Kevin] Gilbert. One of the panels featured three young white male poets reading from and talking about the influences on their own poetics. During question time, Fogarty wanted to know why all three were writing on and through European poetic traditions. Why weren't they writing about what was going on in Australia?

Adopting Fogarty's own position we need to ask: what would it mean to read Australian poetry from within a tradition closer to the poetry itself? I cannot speak of Murri intellectual life in relationship to Fogarty, but for Australian poetry it might mean attending to Alice Moyle, Stan Grant, Faith Bandler, Noel Pearson, Bill Neidjie, Banjo Clarke, Ruby Langford, John Passmore, Robin Boyd, Paddy Roe, Wayne

King, AB Original, Kev Carmody, Doris Pilkington Garimara, Xavier Herbert, Alexis Wright, Mary Durack, Donald Stuart, Donald Norman, Peter Coppin, Bill Harney, A.P. Elkin and a whole corpus of intellectual work rather than reading much of the contemporary theory that is applied to poetry at the moment.

The featurist instrumentalising of theory is a tendency common to much reviewing and essay writing here. But, what might recognition of local philosophy mean for local poetics? That matters for poetry if only because the bounds of Australia need be questioned in discourses of our own making. The belief to overturn is that we have no discourse, that we have no language, that we have only words but no ecosystem is common.

In response to Toby Fitch's question of whether he spoke any other languages, John Tranter replied:

> Just English. I have always felt that Australians are lucky to have the English language, with its extraordinary reach and complexity, most of which comes from the cross-fertilisation with other languages, because of Britain having been invaded and conquered by the Celts in 600 BC, by the Romans in 43BC, by the Anglo-Saxons in AD 450, by the Vikings in 793, by the Norman French in 1066 and by the Dutch under William of Orange in 1688. The last is often overlooked, but it was a massive invasion of 53 warships bristling with 1,700 cannon, which fortunately was not resisted and in many cases welcomed, at least by those of a Protestant persuasion.

I agree that Australia is lucky to have English. And yet,

rich as this history is, we need to remember that we are also lucky for all the other languages that are here, including the ones that are still being made. This might include a unique Australian lingo, which could simply be a performative hope based upon a distinguishing social morphology, lexicon, apparatus, and, of course, history of the continent.

Over the course of my life, I have taken classes in Mandarin, Japanese, French, German, Spanish and Hindi. I have varying capacities in each of them and am trying to develop my vocabulary in some Western Pilbara languages. But, what is interesting is how they are porous. We cannot think about 'breaking' language if we do not think about what being 'broken' means and what enables theory, as pieces of language games, to shift homegrounds. For the unfamiliar, 'bonjour, j'aime le croissant' may be easier to understand than Paul Celan's 'Todesfugue', but for the defamiliar the opposite might be true, which is why one imagines the statement that 'poetry is all French to me'. This is not only about using the master's language against him, but about constructing a different game, a suburb that makes a city new in its oldness such that one 'player' may seek to become a game themselves. Theory is one of those languages that often obeys a whole logic to separate it from the ordinary. We have not fallen out of theory unless we begin to see through it ourselves and begin to fall deeper into it.

For example, and in adopting and subverting one crumb of the Marxist lexicon, rather than seeing 'the alienated' as turning into a objectified worker (say a depressed celebrity) which implies that the abstraction of social relations is negatively privileged, one may argue for the freedom that comes with chosen, intentionalised ritual play. Ritual stands against the market precisely because of a dialectical relationship of frame, which is not to say the slave has unrealised power over the master necessarily, but that the poet can experience ontological transcendence (freedom) when they succeed in the deep abstraction of language creation. Intention undoes habitus. Ritual opposes market. Speaking tongues is not only the task of the translator, but the role of the poet in seeing through what English is and towards the universal language itself. It is about achieving a higher synthesis between lingo and theory.

After all, *if the grass is always greener why not look to the sky?*

Grass needs sky to grow even as grass gives sky something to do. When we realise that, we might not think about how broken the system is, but that we can create no system at all in an intellectual poetics for this continent.

11

Presented as Being There

Critique might console itself with 'anti-capitalism' or 'anti-neoliberalism', but it is hard to envisage the ends of those ideological persuasions precisely because we neither have utopias to believe in or because of the ego attachment of the author who trades in any particular fetish commodity, both of which prevent a truer consciousness. This is not to point out, pedantically, that we are all complicit as if that were a reason to trade in weapons. It is to argue against the congealed ideologies that are now ascendant amongst intellectuals, including poets. That Communism was once an envisioned alternative should be salutary but not because it offered an out, but because in the specific interactions of past geopolitics we might begin to unpack consciousness itself. History as a philosophy provides some sort of consolation if not answer.

With the end of history, the fall of the Wall, and the rise of state capitalism, we do not need to necessarily let go of our structural dreams, but to re-jig them slightly. Indeed, shoring up the belief in non-violence as the social articulation of a poetic life might encourage us to find a way through the morass of leaps forward, central planning and revolution, which might also go by the names of boom, efficiency, jobs and growth. The answer then is all around us even as we do not know how to name it so.

That is why I do not accept payment for my poetry. That this comes at financial cost to me is not what I want to highlight, but that in the process of giving away poetry I launder money. If one thinks the only way to value add is to turn nature into commodity, then one needs to recognise the possibility of making trade clean through the cessation of money. This is the gift economy.

Precisely because no one gets paid and there is a lingering belief in romantic self-expression, poets often make the mistake of thinking that their fellows are friends rather than colleagues, or maybe even enemies, who trade in obligatory gifts. That might go part of the way to explaining why rifts are so common – people have assumptions about relations because, paradoxically, we are all in this together even as it is intensely fought. That is about misrecognising relations as social rather than economic. As Marcel Mauss writes:

> … in this system of ideas one gives away what is in reality a part of one's nature and substance, while to receive something is to receive a part of someone's spiritual essence. To keep this thing is dangerous, not only because it is illicit to do so, but also because it comes morally, physically and spiritually from a person. Whatever it is … it retains a magical and religious hold over the recipient. The thing given is not inert. It is alive and often personified, and strives to bring to its original clan and homeland some equivalent to take its place … Men say that gift-exchange brings abundance of wealth.

The gift is qualitatively different from the commodity

exchanges that occur in society nowadays. That is what makes it dangerous and subversive. That poetry is run on the smell of an oily rage is a well-known fact. In today's Australia, poets are the most poorly paid of any of the writing professions. As David Throsby, Jan Zwar and Thomas Longden write:

> The highest average earnings from practising as an author *for the top 25%* of authors are associated with education authors ($16,500), followed by children's authors ($14,000) and genre fiction authors ($11,100). The lowest average earnings received by the top 25% of earners are associated with poets ($4,900).

This does not include the unpaid, bureaucratic labour in the poetry economy – editorial, logistical and marketing work often happens without financial compensation. Poets do rumble about this but why should we assume that payment is a good thing? To think of it thus is to assume not only money's primacy as a form of recognition – my work is worth something because it is valued in dollars – as well as a failure to think, in utopian terms, of how social relations may indeed be different because of the economy as a whole. That is to say, commodities, including books, might not only abstract and alienate because of their circulation but might also empathise and generate if they are post-money, which is to say, a gift. That we reserve this type of exchange for birthdays, Christmas and other festivals not only points us towards where people potentially feel happiest, but also how we might consume in a way that encourages positive emotional bonds. This is not to deny the obligations that are established by gift giving, the fact that we expect to have it reciprocated even as we might not ever get that chance.

The gift would have us believe, rightly in a vulgar way, that there is an outside of capitalism because there is an outside of money. For me, this takes the form of poetry, which is a precious exchange, and only offers an example of the labour many people already perform unconsciously. The task of poetics is to bring that consciousness into language and in so doing understand how we might better know our selves and give that to the world as a hopeful dream devoid of ideology.

12

Renewing Localism

The boundaries of Australia are porous and multiple and heuristic; five hundred countries, thousands of suburbs, various islands, all places we can travel to without a legal passport but needing some sort of confidence and material to pass from one place to another. There are bodies that have come from all over to be here and we live in imagined collectives whose possibilities are yet to be fully realised. In poetry today these bodies include Tanya Thaweeskulchai, Adolfo Aranjuez, Lian Low, Bella Li and Ellen Van Neerven. And those bodies have a legitimate political positionality with accumulated capital in safe subcultural spaces, and so they should given our historical marginalisation. But what then, in a liberal identity politics era, does renewing localism mean?

Let me start by saying that my locale is different from yours, but in the basis of that difference we can find solidarity rather than tear each other apart. This is precisely because we see ourselves as autonomously enabled rather than colonised. Local to me means my self – where have I been and what have I done? It is a micro-historical question that engages with structures. For you it might be important that I have Malayalee parentage if we wish to connect as people of colour or Indians or immigrants; for you it might matter that

I grew up in the suburbs and so we can connect on the basis of our upbringing and lifestyle; it might matter that I have been through an educational institution and hold degrees that allow me to write in this way; or you may like the fact that I have worked in remote Indigenous communities and attended traditional law ceremonies in sovereign countries on this continent.

But all these differences, 'intersectionalities', of my identity can be used as methods and tools from which to reach out a hand of friendship rather than erect the false idea that I am distinct. I, which is one of the most misleading words in the language, means you to some degree because it is in Others that we see ourselves. We see ourselves as a function of social relations, which is necessary precisely because we are social beings. We see this most clearly in the body, which is imprisoned by the soul, and how we breathe the same air even as we have lungs that are our own, connected though they are to the outside world. When we say 'mine' we not only mean earth that is dug from under our feet but our body's own. My locale begins in this mine.

The question of renewing localism means not only renewing Australia, given that this is a neat confidence trick of abstraction, but also that we renew our selves. The Australia we need to renew is not only Ngunnawal or Kulin country, but also the infrastructure that floats on top of them. By saying this, I do not mean that we should reify our current tropes, but that in order to forge a future worth living we must relate as collaborators from a place that is regional and international. Our audience must be the world from where we stand, two feet in salt or sand or granite. Nor must we conflate an anti-capitalist or anti-globalisation polis to be one where we remain cousins to metropolitans with ethical engagement. In doing so, we have failed to come to terms with how we take a position, falling into paradigms neither of our own making and those that seem tired, boring and boneheaded but also not tired, boring or boneheaded enough. What is the path to take?

That differs for everyone, but I want to draw attention to the work of ethnomusicologists like Sally Treloyn, Linda Barwick, Alan Marritt as well as the wide variety of locally managed Indigenous language centres such as Wangka Maya. When we are encouraged to see this work as aesthetic rather than anthropological we will start to engage with the bedrock of language here in this place.

But it is there too in other artistic expressions, including the foraged food movement from Rene Redzepi's *Noma* to Magnus Nilsson's *Fäviken*. Closer to home, Paul Iskov's *Fervor* is a roaming feast that draws on knowledge from traditional owners and remote communities to create a clear expression of a high, connected and focused aesthetic that teaches us a certain poetry in what is always already here. My argument in renewing localism is not about renewing the nationalist frame of reference. In other words, the construction of an 'Indigenous experience' as the *ur* origin fails conceptually because it is not the Noongar experience, the Ngarluma experience, the Arrernte experience, all of which are neither similar nor singular, and instead 'the Indigenous' may simply lock us into a false binary consciousness. It is not necessarily an identity construction that comes from the ground up.

One of the things we must do in renewing localism is relearn empire and our own places in it. We might like to conflate the empire with 'America' or 'Europe', but this is not specific enough. We might like to fight capitalism, but my critique of it simply asks what does that mean? Do we mean the unshackled market, do we mean consumerism, do we mean commodity fetishism? Do we mean all of the above?

All these are questions that need be debated in the process of coming to an agreeable set of terms despite the fact that one can gain capital and energy from their deployment. For the 'English' language, I may locate the Queen at the centre of a set of radial relations that emanate from her crown, and her tongue. In that sense, it is about retraining the senses – how can we look and acknowledge traditional representation of Wardan, Alyawarre, Dharawal poetics; what does it means to see and learn from the public resources in Australian Institute of Aboriginal and Torres Strait Islander Studies; how can we look and get the diversified vision or the world, which speaks back to all the peoples who live here, be they from Pintupi or Punjab country; how can we see our suburbs differently by re-reading Robin Boyd and Howard Arkely in light of Rover Thomas and Reko Rennie? Those are the questions for a poetics that is local to our selves and immanent now.

13

Southern Ethnopoetics

It is an axiom of thought called 'ancient' that all things are connected (Plato, *Dao DeChing, Bhagavad Gita*); and though this belief exists in recent writers from Paul Ehrlich to Michel Foucault, it would be more commonplace to argue that in our 'modern' era we are compartmentalised, segmented, separate. That might simply be the first myth of the alienated self, a self that seeks re-enchantment, through drum circles, through whole foods, through an economy of techniques that get us back to the natural.

That modernity has been intimately tied up with nature, and its guardians (the 'primitive' and 'native'), is illustrated in the canvases of Pablo Picasso and Paul Gauguin, the tongues of *Aimé Césaire* and D.H. Lawrence, and Sigmund Freud's theories of totem and taboo. This is hardly less the case when one gets closer to the frontier as lived experience in a more recent age be that the Amazon of Werner Herzog or the Patagonia of Bruce Chatwin. What is today's Australian to do? What are 'we' to make of a resource, archive, material that has been exploited by influences that might actually thwart our 'national development' precisely because of reigning paradigms and the congealed sediment of history?

After all, as R.D. Fitzgerald wrote in 'An Attitude to Modern Poetry':

> Southern poetry has its own tradition, and actually should not be considered against the background of contemporary overseas movements, but in its own place within the framework of the older English tradition.

Fitzgerald's attempt to move away from 'Australia', if only to reinscribe it within another national tradition ('English' not British), was also a move away from the sociology of poetics ('not contemporary'). This is to say nothing of how his view may not actually be a simple Anglophonia precisely because the English tradition could be said to be polymorphous and assimilative all at once.

It strikes one if only because of today's transnational bent – poets who go overseas for reading tours, critics who study interstitial spaces and exchanges, publishers who have no fixed address. But Fitzgerald's move – to disentangle Australia from 'the Southern' and return it to English – is altogether different from the newer desire to tangle Australians in 'the South', precisely because the latter relocates tradition away from hegemonic authority. Now, it is not *au fait* to advocate that Judith Wright belongs in a world canon precisely because the canon has been sunk. This is not to disregard the classics or to flatten hierarchies as if on a dry plain, but to comment on what has happened thanks to post-colonials be that Gayatri Spivak or Edward Said, Chinua Achebe or Ngũgĩ wa Thiong'o. The classics do indeed have a place in the world of world literature. The lamb *has* entered the dreaming and might be said to be a globetrotting trope nowadays. The wombat on the other hand has scarcely entered the imagination at all.

What this means is not that our poetry in Australia need abound in 'local flavour' or become a network of easily recognised signs, which themselves attest to a history of postmodern if 'grand' tradition, but that the individual must create a lexicon that is fabular, proverbial, vernacular. That way it may travel from me to you. I do not mean this as the romance of legends, of a 'modern' nostalgia for songlines be they a religious techne of the self. This would be to simply misapprehend the fact that they are not 'our' sediment from which we could go no further or deeper. We need to learn that there are no answers at all, merely more questions, questions that the classics, and minor poems alike, ask of us as long as we read them right.

Without this historical re-examination of political and cultural complexities that open up an awareness of our understanding of the self and other, we will languish in a 'modern' consciousness that occludes a closeness to a truer state, which is not to say our natural one. Poetics history is not only the story of how poets suffer other poets from their past (as well as their contemporary network), but also how they enjoy collaboration with the guiding light of societies as ecosystems. That this is enmeshed with the paradoxical pleasure of forces that labour to erase, negate, devalue us *as poets* means that how we do history as well as what, where, why and who writes and sings continues to matter for our lives today. Of this we might say as Ysola Best, Candace Kruger and Patrice O'Connor do in *Yagambeh Talga*:

Kambullum wongara
Woojerie bingging
Woodooroo wongara
Woojerie kunneng

When the silky oaks are in bloom, the turtles are fat.
When the tea trees are in bloom, the mullet are fat.

14

New Mimicry

Recently, I took a public servant friend of mine who has an American Green Card and works in social cohesion at the Commonwealth Department of Justice to a poetry reading. Afterwards he asked me why they all spoke with American accents.

I said to him, 'What do you mean?'

He said: 'They all sounded like they were from the Mid-West, that kind of newsreader voice, not as serious but still. There was also that guy with the hip hop thing.'

'I didn't hear that.'

But the next time I heard poetry live I noticed the accent, which has indeed become Americanised. When I say *become* what do I mean? Compared to the older generation, even those from 1968 who were influenced by Donald Hall's *New American Poetry*, today's young Australian poets sound positively Yankee.

What does this say about mimicry? Have we simply changed masters from a pukkah BBC Queen's English to a benign soft power celebrity from Chicago via Hollywood or the Upper East Side? It needs to be acknowledged that there is a class, race and geographic texture to voice here, which often circulates in some imaginary bourgeois, white, urban world. Although many here do not seem to consciously try to become like W.B. Yeats or Kurt Schwitters or Saul Williams, there is a generic imitation. Voice is individual after all, but accent is not. And America, or a subsection of it, is part of our culture industry *lingua franca* from movies to podcasts to television. It might not be traceable to other poets at all. Surely, the kids watch *Survivor* more than they listen to PoemTalk? The imitation my friend highlighted comes out in all of poetry's aspects and not just the oral.

For many, imitation is the poorest of all the arts. In the estimation of Plato it is for mere 'idol worshippers'. But if mimicry is also the sincerest form of flattery, we might want to say that the best imitator is a flatterer who fools even the philosopher, which might be no bad thing. We might also have to distinguish what type of mimicry is valuable, good, and even original.

Cultural appropriation – of form, of voice, of content – is seen as the negative form of mimicry, the technique that draws the ire of people in social media, newspapers and water cooler chat. It would seem like the exploitation of the weak. However, what is negative depends on context and not all appropriations are equal regardless of what the baying crowd suggests. In *Poetic Questions,* Proclus suggests that the reason poets are not allowed in Plato's Republic is, firstly, about the problem with imitation; secondly, about the 'unlimited moving of the passions'; and thirdly, 'saying any sort of wickedness to gods and heroes'. In other words it is about cultural appropriation, too much emotion and irreverence. Today, that might mean the sterotypers are as bad as the Twitter frenzy of the correctly liberal set. And yet, to say as much is to be irreverent toward a reigning paradigm of ideology that apparently safeguards rights.

Is the best form of mimicry simply the one that targets power, which is to say a type of mimicry that engages the civil faculty? Is it that which self-consciously undoes the American newsreader through mocking or does this simply lock the young poet into a dialectic from which there is no escape? What might be the power in mimicking the object (the actual white body hence whitening cream) or that of the spirit (the idea of the whiteness and its invisibility and privilege)? Or is one of these worse because no matter what we regard as 'higher' might mean a greatest distance to fall?

Of course, I myself am a fallen man, not from the Garden, but from somewhere, perhaps simply from my historic self if not in the eyes of the world. I will always be that person. But this neither stops me from becoming knowledgeable of poets in Othered categories, or from being a good interlocutor precisely because I, like all people, have a capacity for empathy. That we might imagine our selves as their selves is only the start. That these identities and poetries are multiple, shifting, intersectional should not then be used for isolating individuals precisely because we do not know the whole story and also because constructing the new utopia might be better thought of as a creative pursuit that relies on a type of negation not defined by a language of our choosing. There is always complicity. There is no ideal person who speaks only against privilege; there is no disembodied poetics that has a pure tongue to speak back against empire, misogyny or history. But, there are allies and preferences.

For when we examine the life of any one individual we see their effects and enmeshment, which, because it is life, escapes full illumination in poetics and writing even as it may serve an artistic and political purpose. That we like to think we are better than the past, that we do not repeat kitsch, and cannot discern the distinction between a biscuit tin with parrots and the politically incorrect iconography, imagery and narrative of our precursors, be that the warrior holding a spear standing on one leg or the white housewife tending to her oven, means that in failing to find a Historic Voice we fail to find our own historic voice after all. That might mean the presence, however sedimented, of a Susannah Carr or Rick Ardon, a Dennis Commetti or Leila Gurruwiwi. Whatever it is, activist listening will enable us to listen better to ourselves and be newsworthy for whatever term we make sense of now.

15

Politicising Conceptualism

There are few poets working in Australia that adhere to conceptual methods in a similar way to Americans such as Kenneth Goldsmith, Vanessa Place, Erin Morrill, Craig Santos Perez, Myung Mi Kim, Dawn Lundy Martin, Douglas Kearney, Jeremiah Rush Bowen or Joey Yearous-Algozin. Although there are notable poems that use uncreative and other conceptual methods, Australian poets are not primarily known for those pieces. And so, one could be forgiven for assuming that conceptualism does not have a firm basis down under. But this is altogether unravelled by the uncreative language acts that have not yet been framed as poetic as well as amateur acts that have yet to adequately pierce official verse culture. We might not have *Day* down under but we certainly have daily newspapers and it might simply be about critiquing uncreatively to allow us to view Australia less as a site of potential and more as a site of actualisation. This continent is not an island or a shadow.

An Australian poetry, and poetics, that took seriously its own conceptualism might be somewhat different than the dominant American mode and for this we could look more to the spirit of poetry. However, such a proposal rests on a particular sociological conception of representation here rather than on a distinctly aesthetic idealism of the place.

To think through a native conceptualism that seems less like another imported paradigm indicative of an insecure, mimetic cultural cringe requires unpacking what is possible in today's Australia.

Australia is for the most part monolingual and, as other critics have made clear, overwhelmingly white in terms of its 'recognised', poetic community. To be certain, this is challenged by the cultural diversity of spoken word performance as well as the proliferation of Indigenous poetries that escape attention in the academy and published discourse. Despite the determination and self-sufficiency of poetry as a sub-cultural status group there is neither the idea of a perceived tradition akin to the United Kingdom beyond two hundred years or the critical mass of the United States. But conceptualism in the context of English language nations remains important. Conceptualism in Australia needs to re-integrate its politics so it can adequately embrace the paradox that it decreases American influence and yet readily accepts its innovations. This is not about the eclecticism and the personal choice of the reader and what America they choose, and hence seeing this as a school of influence that is liberally liberating. It is about the realisation that what makes Australia unique in the world has a political implication.

Conceptualism here needs to take seriously a critique of 'America', but also the utopian possibilities of a settler society ravaged by violence and benignly progressing towards an increasingly same same vision of the future. This is not a project advocating one re-type American texts and subvert them by biography, or indeed appropriate Indigenous cultures in a Jindyworobak project for the conceptual age. It is about responding to the aesthetics of engagement that considers the discourse of politics in daily life as it is experienced. There must be a realisation too, even far too late in this piece, that poetry is ill confined by the nation, which means we must sing the Internationale for pacifism while retaining optimism in the possibilities of the state itself.

What this might look like is not so much a #workingonmynovel, but a #libspill. This is to say nothing of extending the lessons of conceptualism, and indeed post-conceptualism and pre-post-conceptualism, to experiences that are politically significant (even or especially including how politics matters on the ground in vote getting, policy, legislation). If gendering and racing the project was one such avenue popular in America, re-discovering the state as a utopian possibility may be one way we can think through and against what has all too often been a simplified imperial project.

16

Invisible Ink

Although I have written poetry for over a decade, it was only recently that I toiled in the poetry bureaucratic apparatus. I use the term 'poetry bureaucratic apparatus' to mean its administrative wing – organising readings, promoting prizes, reading submissions, applying for grants, editing posts, doing social media, paying poets. This bureaucratic apparatus is for the most part *ad hoc*. There is no union, no enterprise bargaining agreement, no industrial relations body, no governing organisation. It is, of course, simply one aspect of the gift economy that is poetry. For six months, I held a paid position at Australian Poetry, which could be regarded as the closest thing to a peak body for poets. It is as establishment as it gets outside the university, which is only confirmed by its location inside the Wheeler Centre in Melbourne.

However, as a multicultural, mixed race, hybrid person I was often struck by how white poetry was there. My daily work routine, my colleagues, the modes of address, the unconscious collective, the self-perception, or lack thereof, presented as white. Not often does this whiteness present itself as 'whiteness'. It is one of whiteness' great abilities to be invisible and in so doing claim to be universal. I do not by any means want to tar everyone with the same brush or to think that whiteness disqualifies fellow travellers. Many of my friends are white. Many of my family are too. And I am, in some ways, as well. And yet one can't help but notice that one is surrounded by white faces when one goes to events, when one has meetings, when one walks into the office, when one looks at programming.

We could identify a type of whiteness operating in Australia today, which often glosses its relationship to other hierarchies (class, gender, education) and fails to realise its own structural exclusivity. It is an cross-section of mutually reinforcing privilege that matters for elites in any field. This is the opposite of solidarity. By not actively campaigning to change the raced dynamics of the poetry establishment, I am reminded of Joan Kirner when she said:

> Just by making a decision to stay out of politics, you are making the decision to allow others to shape politics and exert power over you. And if you are alienated from the current political system, then just by staying out of it, if you do nothing to change it, you simply entrench it.

These words are not only salutary for 'poets of colour' but also for those whose identity is complex. 'We' should be in solidarity with marginalised peoples because that is what is valuable. After all, I myself have passed as a white man for most of my life. I have a name – Robert Wood – that is invisible in the hegemonic Anglo society of suburban Australia. I have a body that if a little tanned, a little hook nosed, a little 'Latin' or 'Mediterranean', is nevertheless unthreateningly, benignly unnoticeable. I present in dress and language as white.

But my mother is brown. She and my aunts came to

Australia when the White Australia Policy ended in 1974. Some of them were early international students at universities; others came and began work straight away. Their story over the last forty years resonates with the known narrative of migration – hard work, education, opportunity – and they have, in their own definition, been successful. But their story also has its particular idiosyncrasies and challenges.

I myself knew I was not quite white from very early on. My mother's family, from midnight to caramel to café au lait, was a chocolate box of brownness. There were gingers and blondes and brunettes in my father's family, but mum's made me realise that diversity is skin deep. It was home to me. It still is.

In thinking through identity, in thinking through what I am, I am first led towards clichés. The phrase that seems to be deployed most often is 'walking in two worlds'. In Australia, this is used particularly often for Indigenous people, but one can discern it in post-colonial conversations too. I have a *mata mata* brother-in-law who is half Ngarluma (Aboriginal) and half white (Irish, French, Scottish). Although people no longer use this phrase, he, like me on a different axis, is a 'half-caste'. We could be forgiven for thinking that 'we walk in two worlds'. In a more intellectual iteration, this might be 'hybrid'. But there has always been a little bit of curry in Scotland, always a little bit of whiskey in Kerala. Water connects us all. We are in one world still, even if we can code switch at will.

Passing, of course, has a long and complicated global history including for African American communities, for Anglo-Indian people, for Indigenous Stolen Generations. Colouredness used to be a secret to keep hidden because there were material advantages to presenting as white and less tolerance of us as raced. That has most certainly changed due partly to the end of the White Australia Policy, Civil Rights, self-determination, 'black is beautiful', United Colours of Bennetton as well as the material opportunities afforded to Othered subjects by a whole host of cultural, economic and political changes. But given the political climate, our advances seem threatened, which worries me as a person of colour and a white ally working for solidarity and justice.

Indeed, in other conditions, conditions of my own making, I do see myself as a white man. It is not without some hesitation that I identify as such, if only because being a white man is only half my story. It matters to me though and speaking from the inside, what white men fail to see, what is invisible to all but the extremist fringes, are their forms of group solidarity, their shared experiences of the body, their political position as collective rather than as individual subjects. If us poets of colour have historically been stereotyped and viewed as a group lacking individual identification, white men have rejoiced in the opposite.

That poets of colour are still not proportionally represented in books, festivals, panels is not mere oversight, but systematic and structural. And this matters for the art. Where would we be without Elena Gomez, Kim Cheng Boey, Ouyang Yu, Sudesh Mishra or Ivy Alvarez? The sea change, a veritable flood that has occurred in Australian poetry over the last ten years is remarkable, but for it to falter now would be a disservice to the art itself. Identities matter. Experiences matter. And our poetics needs to reflect that.

17

The New Reality in Australian Poetry

The generation of Murray is not my generation. The generation of Adamson is not my generation either. Nor is it Tranter or Kinsella. My generation is a new generation in Australian poetry. We are 'emerging'. In this era of the 'contemporary', particularly as a political proposition after the end of history, it is a dangerous endeavour to suggest there is a modernist / socialist realist debate. And while the actors have undoubtedly changed (as has the world and its labels) we can discern two such realities in the newest generation of Australian poets. These poets are working in 're-formed realism' and 'sentimental radicalism'.

I take as foundational in the modernist / socialist realist debate the division that emerged in World War Two and was later embodied by Katharine Susannah Prichard and Dorothy Hewett in the field of Australian poetry. Of course, one could look to György Lukács and Theodor Adorno for similar faultlines, or to Albert Tucker and Neil Counihan, but given my position on Noongar country it is important to see what sediment exists here. This is a genealogical and sociological position, not a search for roots or an importation of culturally sanctioned and accumulated references.

Both modernism and socialist realism are important unconscious aesthetic influences in today's new generation of Australian poets. This is simply one way of organising these groups. It is a poetics of critique and projection, not an inalienable and incontestable truth. If one chose to, one could organise the whole in a different way; for example, somewhat predictably, by authorial identity. I would welcome that if only to see how allegiances shift and groups coalesce around different stories. But authorial identity is a red herring and poor analytical tool at the best of times. It ultimately displays a myopic liberalism in the reigning paradigm of identity politics that focuses on the life rather than the art, and fails to come to terms with the death of the author.

That modernism and socialist realism haunt Australian poetry now seems to be in their complicated historical positions. They have not left living relatives but ghostly spectral presences. This is no doubt due to the elasticity of their original definitions and the catholic breadth of today's poets.

The nationalist moment has well and truly passed, but networking language now means some possibility of return to a division that operated before. My generation works as bowerbirds do, taking language from all over to make its nest. The American influence that is predominant would seem to be John Ashbery and L=A=N=G=U=A=G=E in re-formed realists, and hip-hop in sentimental radicals. But this does not change the fact that they speak in a distinctly Australian idiom.

As Bernard Smith wrote in 1944's 'The New Realism in Australian Art', 'the development of this realist tendency from the ranks of the moderns should be distinguished from the rise of modernism itself'. Indeed, there may be poets working in a modernist vein but the re-formed realists have taken modernism and twisted it, which is not entirely separate from a socialist realist iteration. This is particularly so in Bonny Cassidy's *Final Theory*, Corey Wakeling's *Goad Omen* and Luke Beesley's *Jam Sticky Vision*. These three poets seem to be the most prominent exponents of this style, which is characterised by disrupted narrative, concern with daily life and intermedia, and experimentation from a centripetal location. It could be said to have a stronghold in Giramondo's list. But this is complicated by their publication of Lachlan Brown and Fiona Wright who seem to work in an entirely different, and altogether more suburbanist iteration. As Smith suggests 'to accept realism is not to retreat', which is to say it is not a retreat from the treatment of form nor of the figurative world. In the poets mentioned above one is struck by the combination of difficult abstraction and literal image that seems to explode the binary oppositions that so animated mid-century visual artists.

As Gertrude Langer wrote in 'Notes for a Talk on Modern Art and Abstraction' from 1945:

> To abstract is to distil and to distil is to *intensify*.
> The contemporary artist (the genuine ones
> anyhow) search for an essence, a central
> meaning in what is seen. One group of
> abstract artists consciously abstracts (or distils
> from nature). The other group does not but,
> ultimately, no one can get away from nature,
> even if it is not so obvious in the work.

Upon first inspection the sentimental radicals might appear to be moving away from nature, such is their relatively urban coordinates, but this is simply to resurrect an unhelpful city-bush divide that does nothing to comment on the animating energy and form of the work. The importance of this passage is, I think, in highlighting *intensification*. Emerging from a context of spoken word, slam and orality, one notices the desire the intensify experience in the work of sentimental radicals like Omar Musa, Benjamin Solah and Maxine Beneba Clarke. Their content is avowedly political, they deal in ordinary language and have a proclivity for rhyme, but this is not combined with a formal experimentation common to re-formed realists. However, one notices in them a willingness to try new things and to be influenced by shared innovations, hence the break in strict teleological linearity common to the generation as a whole. Modernism matters here as well.

In splitting hairs, re-formed realism tends to be concerned with the form politics takes, which means it sides with a Hewettian archetype. By contrast, sentimental radicalism takes a political content (the Prichard mode). Rather than a traditional dialectics being projected, I would think of them in a synchronic sub status group conflict given their temporal concurrence. Who is the master and who is the slave remains to be seen as the politics paradigm means there are shifting intersectionalities that make the assessment of power a fraught endeavour, particularly if it aspires to thoroughness. In addition, accessing information on the history of the book (sales, advances, reviews) and its performance (door takings, audiences, launches, readings, festivals) makes it harder to assess the field comparatively and to define where a poet definitively stands. While any poetics must always historicise, we must also always contextualise and in so doing understand that the frame will determine the weight, gravity, importance, power, place and so forth. And yet, one might choose to see ΠO as their common antecedent. This is not first order obvious, and I doubt many count him as a great influence. He matters for his synthetic rejection of Hewett and Prichard, for his epics which are poems including *local* history, and for his formal inventiveness and orality/publication combined. He is decidedly his own thing, which was also decidedly a new thing at the time.

What unites my generation is a lack of politicised coherence rather than an agreeable third way middle ground, which accounts for the majoritarian politics of poetry as a whole. Re-formed realists forget the content or, rather, abstract the content for fear of didacticism and obviousness. Sentimental radicals forget the form, meaning that the radicalism of previous generations has not found its successor and that there is a formal conservatism that seems, at its worst, like the continued singing of the Internationale. This is despite the fact that the old can become new again, and that tradition is necessary for the revolutionary activities of tomorrow. It would be skulduggery and numbskullery to suggest otherwise. However, there is a half committed politics in a great many poets of my generation. This is not to deny the importance of a personal ideology grounded in embodied experience, but it is to acknowledge the decline of party membership and the lack of policy vocabulary. We are all Marxists now but none of us are members of the Communist Party.

This observation does not prevent seeing that some individuals are both poet and activist. Omar Sakr is one example. He is not alone in this, even if he is exemplary, and seems the opposite of what Albert Tucker suggested of his contemporaries when he said:

> The function of the artist is interpreted as that of a glorified cartoonist and banner maker … Only political action has validity today. Therefore art

> can only achieve validity when it functions in a direct and immediate political sense. It must be socially utilitarian consciously carrying out a correct political duty. Art is only art when it is politics.

Sakr's work is saturated with his authorial politics but this is sophisticated rather than utilitarian. This highlights the fact that we need to interrogate what art and politics are in a fundamental way, especially in our language games that matter materially. This is preferable than simply assuming ideological positions and proceeding as though they were inalienable. In other words, the fundamentals need always to be questioned.

For re-formed realism and sentimental radicalism one need turn to 'The Antipodean Manifesto' to suggest that 'if the triumph of the non-figurative art in the West fills us with concern so too does the dominance of social realism in the East'. There are, of course, different ways to this, and these are evident even in specific poems by the poets named above which undo this dated if paradigmatic assertion, complicating further my analytical critical enterprise (see the prose of Beesley for example).

If the threat to the species in the modernist / socialist realist era was a communal suicide through the nuclear bomb, now it is a slow burn asphyxiation via carbon poisoning. It would not be a stretch to assume all the poets listed in this essay believe in human-caused climate change. If we take seriously the threat of global warming (which is already a lived reality for those positions of precariousness called 'bare life') we must ask ourselves: what is the point of poetry? This is not to dismiss the cultivation of beauty or the pursuit of art for art's sake, or the formal abstraction or naïve hopefulness of other poetries now, precisely because all these ambitions can contribute to the coming society. This may be mainly through therapeutic means, which move us toward the necessarily utopian premise of tomorrow, a utopia in negation of apocalyptic visions complete with landslides, cyclones and earthquakes. That might mean acknowledging that the poetries described here, of my generation, is a reflection of the current crisis as well as a solution of sorts. Its possibility as an answer is surely in its *mabarn* and inflected utility rather than pragmatic pronouncements per se.

The revolutionary possibility is in taking seriously a discourse of 'country' as a basis for identification and law/lore. 'Australia' may be moribund but it is not yet bankrupt precisely because we are in Noongar country, Wurundjeri country and more. Country is a bigger concept than nation – deeper, truer, longer, autonomous, sustained. How do we find an ongoing native memorialisation then? I think for that we can turn to David Unaipon when he wrote:

> Perhaps some day Australian writers will use Aboriginal myths and weave literature from them, the same as other writers have done with the Roman, Greek, Norse and Arthurian legends.

Those words still matter now. The separation, bureaucratisation and professionalisation of politics since Hewett-Prichard has meant not only the evisceration of politics by cookie cutter, machine made, grey flannel apparatchiks, but also the siloing and institutionalisation of poetry. It is not enough to say this poem is political; these words are weapons, or vice versa … that this word does not relate to the world. It is necessary to advocate for a poetry and politics that sociologically gauge the material influence, success, importance of the specific linguistic contribution. In other words, how does a sonnet change deaths in custody?

For the most part, poets display a narcissistic and naive politics. At best, an incredibly limited purview and constituency mean that a precious few might be altered by it. What poets do in their extracurricular time is incredibly important. How their private citizenship bleeds into their published (and hence public) language matters. This is partly why, in my generation of Australian poetry, the work Matthew Hall, Natalie Harkin and Michelle Cahill is particularly important. When their influence is more keenly felt, one may be able to better gauge the shape of the world to come. Yet, the reading habits of practical people of action do little to dispel the idea that poetry works at a glacial pace, that it takes two generations for the conceptual to become the functional in Tucker's terms. What *was* innovative in literature becomes the solace or guiding light now, which is seen in Paul Farmer's use of Frederico García Lorca in *Pathologies of Power*, in Bob Brown's use of various poems in *Optimism*, in Barack Obama's use of Langston Hughes in *Dreams of My Father*. This is not to instrumentalise poetry but to observe its utility in fields one would not consider poetic in the first instance.

There will, hopefully, be no end of history. There always was, always will be a struggle to determine our debates and definitions, our fates which find their necessary and charged linguistic expression in poetry of all kinds. We could discern in reformed realism and sentimental radicalism the fault lines of my generation, which is simply one way of reading the present. That we alone should determine our future goes without stating. It might just be necessary to ask who we are to begin with at all.

18

On the Island of Beginnings

He has been thinking of this project the whole time he has been on this island. Although he will be its only true reader, he proposes it to the animals that have become his friends. To the birds, lizards, frogs, fish and mammals he asks about the undertaking and they agree that it is worthwhile. They say,

'You never know what a message in a bottle might do. You must try to communicate.'

In any case, he needs to find a way to spend his time, something that will absorb him, and define his day.

To the owl he asks, 'Why do you fly at dusk?'

And the owl says, 'That is what I do. Why do you ask?'

'I am curious about how I shall go about my task.'

'Write your poem when you find the time. At the end of it, you might be able to fly away.'

With that, he sat down to write his poem.

As he saw it, there were three things that he needed to consider. The first was what he did before the poem; the second what happened during the writing; and the third about what comes after. Each of those three things had three things in them also: concept, structure, method happened before one sat down to the task; letter, page, frame occurred during the composition; and effect, reception and next project after one had sent the poem into the world.

He heard Wombat say to him that he needed to write about himself and his world. That could be his concept, his story to show and not tell. If he lived in a place with a newspaper he might write it out; if he knew of wars in the past, he might chronicle the life of one soldier; if he thought himself a lover, maybe he would write of his affairs; if he had been to hell, he might return and say it is not so bad in the first circle; or he could quite simply speak of the animals and his daily life here on the island. But Wombat knew it best when he said that his concept was the thought that motivates the poem.

He sat and thought about it, thought about how he would put his idea into the poem; that he would have to think more on what it was to share his view of the world given that his voice was hoarse and his paper scarce. He could not draft and draft, but he knew that a strong concept would help him out.

Next, Skink came up to him and asked him about structure, about what sort of form the poem would take. He knew of sonnets and pantoums and villanelles, which he remembered from school before he was lost to this island. But Skink said to him,

'Maybe you need a structure that only you know about. Why not something with only vowels? Or some sort of constraint in how you write your poem down?'

He said to Skink: 'You might be right. I might limit the number of lines I write and build a house.'

'You need one to live in, so start with a brick, and if you get lonely in your house once it is complete, keep going so you have a suburb, then a country, then a continent. You might be able to imagine a whole other island that we all could live in as well.'

'Build it up from one line to one stanza to one brick to a panel to a wall to a house and so on and so forth?'

'Now you are thinking like a builder. And remember to drink water.'

When he went to the well to refill his bottle Frog said hello. He asked him:

'What do you think about my poem so far?'

'Have you written anything down?'

'Not yet, but I know I need a concept and then a structure.'

'That is a good start, but how about a method too, a way you write your poems.'

'You don't think I can just sit and imagine words and then share them with you?'

'You might do that, but you could do other things too.'

He realised now that he had seen words written down – in the caves nearby, in the books that lay in his trunk, in the smoke in the air. He would write through other people, he would make his words like ghosts and shadows. That would be his method. It could be like the spirit of the mechanical that he remembered so well.

He slept and in the morning woke up to Emu, who had heard of his poem and come by to help.

'You will need a feather my friend, so you have a pen.'

'Why thank you Emu.'

'What letter will you make?'

'I might scratch around for a little bit and see what comes out.'

'I will leave you to it, but practice on the ground.'

He remembered the lessons of his language teacher who held out there was a lesson behind the grammar and the words, who said some things cannot be translated except for translation itself. He thought about that as he made shapes in the dirt. Maybe he would make his own letters, maybe he could make sounds look like different things on the paper. That was when Kangaroo arrived to give him a page.

'That will help, now you can write on something more worthwhile.'

'This is a page that reminds me of a field. I can open it out and put down anything I want. I can cover it all. It is not as big as the ground, but I am thankful for it anyhow. Thank you 'Roo.'

'I look forward to seeing what you produce.'

He realised the day was becoming warmer and that he needed to get something to eat. He went looking for yams and came back to light the fire and have a little feed. Worm popped up and said,

'Are you really going to write this poem friend?'

'Why yes. What else do you suppose I would do?'

'I am not sure, maybe go for a walk, explore, get out a bit.'

'But I have travelled the island round and round. There is nothing else to find out about. I just want to work on this and send it as a message to the world to see if someone will come and find me now.'

'That makes sense. I will bring you some more ink, so you can keep going. But must you really call it a poem? Think of something else you could put next to it. Call it an essay or an epic or a history or a novel, something like that, then maybe I will read it.'

'I think I will still call it a poem. I have the concept, the structure, the method, the letter, the page and now my frame, which is part of the poem anyway. It is the blurb on the cover or the preface, that kind of thing. If it is ok with you I will keep at as a poem but someone great will endorse it.'

'Suit yourself. I will think about what you say.'

With that Worm left, and he ate his yams and went to sleep.

The next day, when you woke up, he began to think what to do with his poem. He wanted it to be read so that all the animals on the island would have some peace of mind, so that they could be entertained and rest awhile. That was the effect that he wished was his. He hoped it would have a wide readership even if there was only one copy. Maybe Bat could take it round, or Eagle. At that moment, Beetle arrived, sparkling in the morning sun. All he said was:

'Are you finished yet? Everyone is asking where it is. We want to see your poem now.'

'I am here, but I cannot let it go, until I know what comes next.'

'Wombat will have an idea. I will get him if you give me a look at what your poem is.'

'That sounds fair.'

He had written a message in a bottle. It was to his future self as much as anyone or any animal, including Beetle. He called it 'On the Island of Beginnings: Becoming Poet':

Concept | Structure | Method
Letter | Page | Frame
Effect | Reception | Next

With that, he went off to breakfast and thought about the rest of his day and what to write next.

19

You Am I

The fetish for the search of influence as answers, and hence originality as an anti-mimicry that privileges an *ur* rupture, fails as common sense Socratic imperative. This is about genealogy not as studies of the Indigenous, but the embodied archiving of reading practices, which are necessarily dialogic, conversational and collaborative. Roots aren't always in the ground and routes aren't always on the road, less travelled or not. To me, Walt Whitman and Paul Celan have been fellow travellers for some time now. They arrived together in my mind in the form of talks, essays, gossip, infrastructure, and, of course, books.

I met them both as more than whispers in 2008. I was studying in Philadelphia at the time and had grown used to crossing the Walt Whitman Bridge on my way to a sublime Persian restaurant in New Jersey that hosted Sufi events. I knew that Whitman's expansive dream, his inclusivity and hope for America, appealed to me being such a long way from home. Celan came to me that summer when I was living in Berlin. Having grown up in the Bauhaus, my uncle had known him (and Adorno, Gottfried Benn, Max Horkheimer). On his shelf were inscribed, signed, first edition copies from Celan (and Pound, T.S. Eliot, Thomas Mann and William Carlos Williams). He was the one who read Celan to me in German.

That I see them as World Historical poets is fair enough given their current reputations, but the particular shades of that and why and how one would read them now are cases yet to be made. That they can shed light on a specific relationship between poet and reader is relevant enough without their contextual importance or their textual significance. A two-line poem that Whitman wrote in 1860, 'To You', consists of the following rhetorical questions:

Stranger, if you passing meet me and desire to speak
to me, why should you not speak to me?
And why should I not speak to you?

Of this passage Edward Hirsch writes in *How to Read a Poem* that 'it seems entirely self-evident to Whitman that two strangers who pass each other on the road ought to be able to loiter and speak, to connect.' But it goes further than that, which is to say, the 'I' is so capricious that it becomes you, that it is America itself. 'Song of Myself' might as well be called 'Song for You Too'. This type of liberalism is so liberal, so all encompassing in its ambition, that it becomes a type of communal hymn. That Whitman was invariably hidebound by a politics of his day, albeit radical, only suggests that he is of his type and time rather than unnecessarily transcendental. In other words, his erasure of Indigenous Americans and his crude depictions of African Americans, amongst other political views 'we' consider travesties, is symptomatic of the late nineteenth century. That one must address the state of the union is not to be denied, but nor should one unduly indict him for the attempt, however significant. That he was an ambulance driver during the Civil War should impress because within his structures he reached for a pacifist possibility that was endearingly humanist.

That Celan was also enmeshed in war is most clearly seen by his perennial representation as *the* witness of the Shoah. Indeed, the poem he is most famous for – 'Todesfugue' – has become the paradigmatic poetic statement of 'the Jewish experience' in World War Two. The fugue, both as a contrapuntal musical phrase and as a psychiatric disorder on the loss of self-awareness, comes from Latin *fuga* meaning 'flight'. And for Celan, this is a flight, a flight from Germany, from the Shoah, from the concentration camp. In the poem, the 'I' is absent, as if, zen-like, one could expel the individual, the witness who wants to disappear but cannot yet. If 'Todesfugue' is a negation of Whitman that shows us a different vision after his ecstatic liberalism, after modernity, after Auschwitz, then we can take Whitman and Celan as dialectical bookends.

What comes after this depends on where one stands but for me that means making sense of global consciousness (moon landing, climate change, United Nations), decolonisation (India, Vietnam, 'Africa') and suburbanisation (car, television, mall). From these organising principles we can regard the necessary context for intelligible poetries that speak with Whitman and Celan as equals. This is the owl that carries with it the message for the 21st century's reader. May it find its place before dawn.

As Celan wrote:

> A poem, as a manifestation of language and
> thus essentially dialogue, can be a message in
> a bottle, sent out in the – not always greatly
> hopeful – belief that somewhere and sometime it
> could wash up on land, on heartland perhaps.

That the owl is a crow, dove or pigeon carrying that

bottle means we can think of country too. If Whitman wrote a celebration for the hope of American future and Celan a lament for the Jewish persecution of the past, then today one might write a rhythm for country as a historian of the present. That some might think of my country as Australia is understandable but in a discourse of my making I would label country as being that of my body – heart, gut, head, if not wispy beard and ashen hair. That country might be 'mulatto', 'half caste', 'mestizo', but whatever it is called, dear reader, dear self of tomorrow, you are always welcome there.

20

Notes on Epic

The closest I ever got to being a formal student of epic was in history class. To be certain, I encountered my fair share of the classics in literature, which included William Shakespeare. If epic came to me through him, in the form of *King Lear*, *Macbeth* or *Hamlet*, it was in a different form than the poem alone. But, history class was where I learnt about all the constitutive parts of epic without recognising the whole. My embrace of it had as much to do with teachers as it did with the subject itself – heroes, tragedy, grandness. But epic in this encounter always placed 'us' as peripheral, which is to say the ANZACS at Gallipoli were only there to help. Perhaps, this is the first lesson to learn – that epic does not happen on a human scale. Even the Trojan War has its fair share of the gods, which are simply figures of congealed myths not unreachable lords. It does not matter if I were told to identify as 'Australian', because in epic, they are always talking about someone else. But in the education system of my suburban primary school, which was aligned with the state, aligned with a public sphere of nation, we learnt about Simpson and his donkey, which seemed idiosyncratic and 'local'.

History at school meant the wars, and there can be no denying that these were on a global scale. The deaths, the thought processes, the absolute permeation of what seemed possible. They connected people right across the globe in a way like never before. This was the case with the Shoah, decolonisation and even the wars on 'our' frontier, billed as they were as a redux of the Great War for civilisation itself. The unconsciousness of history is finding out when to start, is finding out what is the date for the birth of a nation or when the war could be said to have begun. Is it when the declaration is signed? Is it when the first bullet is fired? What is the gun in the cherry orchard that never goes off? How do we start anything at all?

And the answer to this last question determines all the questions that flow from it. For the Annales School the origin is the origin of the world. The architecture is not even archaeological, but so geological that it becomes philosophical. For Foucault, the answer became further and further back as he grew older, the search for answers ending with the Greeks in his *The Care of the Self*. For Roger Chartier, the history of our myths, even in the printing of this book, predate what we like to think of as 'the modern' as that label was a type of the contemporary world that we all think we know and can bring into language so well. The *Bhagavad Gita* would hold that origins are multiple, even if Brahma sits as a fountainhead, and in *Songs of Central Australia,* we come to learn that each place has a beginning that suggests a new historic era that overlaps and encircles our own with a richness that belies our very shallow truths that hope to be universal.

History, like any other discourse, leads us to ask questions, which is a philosophical and critical endeavour. But it also leads us to answers, which is to say creative enterprises that envision a world after the destruction and the gassing. That might be the utopian undertaking that comes from artistic making. In contemporary life, epic has a place at the table. It is there in *Game of Thrones*, but in writing too from Karl Ove Knausgård to Thomas Picketty, who both play to this idea for the crowd as well. But is epic simply 'the big book'? What are the features of epic today? And what might that mean for poetry?

The roots of epic in Australia are historic in the common sense, materialist and secular sense of that designation. This owes much to the structural education system that privileges such possibilities, in whatever congealed, abstracted and instrumentalised form that is. And while *The Odyssey, Iliad, Lusiads, Paradise Lost* and *Divine Comedy* have gods they are nonetheless post-religious in a general way that distinguishes them from *Ramayana, Mahabharata* and the works of Kalidasa. In this way they share something with other settler societies' epic expression, say José Hernandez's *Martín Fierro* or Pound's *Cantos* or Zarilla de San Martin's *Tabaré*, which have, as their rooting origin something 'Western' in the classicist iteration, which does not undo or come to a philosophical understanding of language itself. The question remains, how might one become independent, realised, free, republican, utopian, universal, all from a specific vantage point in a place discursively (mis)constructed as 'Australian'?

This means undoing the sphere of influence as it now stands, which holds fast onto an idea that ideas, and hence epic, come only from the West. What is the appropriate voice for the continent?

Epic is, after all, a continental undertaking, not simply national, but on a scale at least as large as a part of the world that everyone can see, hence Derek Walcott's *Omeros* for the Americas and not simply St. Lucia. I can only speak for myself, but my continent is not aligned with the state as it is currently configured, re-routed as it is by archipelagos on Ngarluma and Noongar country that defy the congealed definitions of 'Australia' itself. There is, of course, a tradition of epic here, one that is private and non-linear, which one cannot appropriate or approximate even if one attends to the inspiration behind it, which might be found in the landforms itself. And from sacred song cycles, which are distinct from *tabi* or *jawi* or *bugarbi* forms, one might want to acknowledge that any epic expression across this continent now must always realise that it is a later arrival.

In my body too, there are the distant bones of coconut groves, of rice paddies and fishing villages, of 'India', or better yet Dravidian or better yet Malayalee classifications. Here, there is the language of birds and oral epics that last all night just like those in country back home. They share in a recent antiquity that is still living, properties and characteristics of the *Cilappatikāram, Manimekalai, Cīvaka Cintāmaṇi, Valayapathi, Kundalakēci*. And one cannot deny the world we have inherited through trade, which brings to us *Beowulf* or *The Faerie Queen*, or *The Song of Hiawatha*. The world is there to be written about from the surrounds of daily life to the vagaries of the imagined field no matter where that takes us. And that is what is possible for the poet working in epic in today's Australia.

And the war we see is the one that matters for epic. Sometimes one does notice the wars that are ongoing, be that the war on terror, on poverty, on drugs, but one cannot help but notice that our elemental debate is between our selves and our nature. And in that, no matter what the epic lens is, one will notice that in crossing the desert or the sea there is always a story to tell in a voice that is all alone and wanting.

21

Place Setting

For the West Australian, Tim Winton and John Kinsella loom large in the literary imagination of today. As novelist and poet they might have a common antecedent in Randolph Stow, who sits behind them in the archive of our Othered coast. Winton has said that to be from here is to be on the 'wrong side of the wrong continent of the wrong hemisphere'. Yet three wrongs do not make a right; two on the other hand – wrong particular, wrong universal – might just be a right philosophy if not quite the philosophy of right. Place – thought of here as a geography that matters in the body with feet on the ground, mind in the sky – matters. That we assume it often contains the 'Australian' is only half of the story, for no matter what category we subscribe to, there are possibilities of freedom. How do we know boundaries, what is inside and outside, especially given that every document of home is also a document of *heimweh*?

The body might be one such location that questions and answers this one. My body looks at home in Cuba, Mexico, Peru, Bolivia, France, Spain, Italy, America, Canada, even Australia. When I am in these places many people assume I am their citizen. And I have been asked by nationals if I am Argentinian, Moroccan and more besides. My body's social place is in a lot of places, and part of that is about being a man with certain privileges. But part of that is about me and my belonging and reception in the world.

I am at home in my body – how can I not be? Yet it has come from places I am not identified with. My sisters and I call Scotland and India home, or even more specifically, Paxton and Anjengo. The first pair of words ties me to a national imperative, ties me to Robbie Burns and Rabindrinath Tagore, and the latter yokes me to our villages where family have lived as far back as anyone can remember. My father keeps a copy of the Burns' poetry by his bedside table, while my mother has *The Home and the World* on her shelf. We know who the local poets are, who the village sages are, the ones drinking whiskey and toddy and talking to all comers in dulcet tones.

When my cousin was married my father recited Burns' 'A Red Red Rose' from memory:

O my Luve is like a red, red rose
That's newly sprung in June;
O my Luve is like the melody
That's sweetly played in tune.

So fair art thou, my bonnie lass,
So deep in luve am I;
And I will luve thee still, my dear,
Till a' the seas gone dry.

Till a' the seas gone dry, my dear,
And the rocks melt wi' the sun;
I will love thee still, my dear,
While the sands o' life shall run.

And fare thee weel, my only luve!
And fare thee weel awhile!
And I will come again, my luve,
Though it were ten thousand mile.

10,000 miles from Scotland is the desert of Australia, land that has 'gone dry', where rocks and dreams of inland seas have indeed 'melted with the sun' even before the realities of climate change began. The desert as distant, and as a place to get away from, is there in Tagore as well, when he writes in 'Where the Mind is Without Fear':

Where the mind is without fear and the head is held
high
Where knowledge is free
Where the world has not been broken up into
fragments
By narrow domestic walls
Where words come out from the depth of truth
Where tireless striving stretches its arms towards
perfection
Where the clear stream of reason has not lost its way
Into the dreary desert sand of dead habit
Where the mind is led forward by thee
Into ever-widening thought and action
Into that heaven of freedom, my Father, let my
country awake

And yet, as a West Australian, the desert is one repository of glorious wisdom, beauty and challenge. It is not 'dreary' or 'dead' at all.

That the synthesis of Burns and Tagores' spirit is to be found in my embodied history is comfort no matter what place I find myself in, no matter where I am writing in San Christobel or San Tropez, and working towards what the best poetic expression of my self might be. I do, of course, have places that I am attached to – Redgate, Wembley, Philadelphia – each being a synecdoche of country, suburb, city. These are about the *ur* places of my memory, grounded in when they first came to me. I know that my country home is Redgate. Here there are crayfish, abalone, herring; white belly frogs, black and red cockatoos, skinks; loam, limestone, karri and cave. I was raised in Wembley looking at bore water stains, dry grass ovals, hills hoists, veggie patches, bungalows and the food court. And the first city I lived in was Philadelphia, home to skyscrapers, subways, street carts, snow, guns, germs and steel.

That I am attached to other locations does not alter the fact of my mythic self-perception of where I grew up. That I can continue to grow does not rely on them in real terms even as they furnish some pleasures that are specific. That is to say, this lexicon of experience interacts with, comes from, adds to, the accepted idea of what is possible in those places. And it is true, it cannot snow in Redgate and one cannot go crayfishing in Philadelphia. But it can 'snow' wherever you want it to, no matter if you are at home or in the world.

As a West Australian, the challenge is to find the universals in our particulars, but this premise starts from the false consciousness that the state is a common experience. The Kimberley is not the Southwest even as one can find Chiko rolls and blue skies in both. Broome is not Kununurra even as one can find mangoes and clouds in both. And so it goes on, becoming more particular and more universal in one and the same term. In cultivating a sense of distinct place one might reach out beyond the conventional network that one initially thinks of. Why can't Wheatlands be next to Cambridge in an embodied mind? Why can't Angelus be next to Paris in another? That they can, and are, is surely one of the beautiful things about being from a country called the poetic imagination, a country that Burns, Tagore and the desert belong to together with many more.

22

Line Break

It is raining. The racers are lined up at the starting line. But poetry is facing the other way. When the gun goes, poetry runs towards the sun while all the others head for the finishing line in the snow.

Homo poeticus is a curious runner for they will head in their own direction often seeking to lose the race before it has even begun. That they then complain when they never really entered at all is a quirk of being a critic inside the same body. And yet, being a critic is an important part of being a citizen in that country called 'language'. It gives one the ability to discern what race one should enter, when the starter's gun will sound, how one finds the finish, why one won. It is nothing short of the philosophical endeavour one can use in deciding if one is a poet in the first place. That might determine what races one allows oneself to enter into.

However, poetry criticism, which is simply to say thinking about poetry, is a marginal pursuit particularly in contemporary Australia. That no poetry critic has won the Pascal Prize, the most prominent national award for any critic, suggests to me that there is something wrong with our sport. There are, of course, many academics that intellectualise poetry including Ann Vickery, Lyn McCredden and Bronwyn Lea. That many of them are also poets should not concern us.

However, my critique of criticism in our day and age is the dire lack of considered public conversation.

With the decline of the radio program *Poetica,* it is left to the circulation of reviews in newspapers and literary journals to maintain a profile of poetics. That mainstream reviews have declined since the 1990s would fuel speculation that 'we' simply do not matter. And yet, there is no meta-thinking on why that is the case by critics. The accusation of navel gazing rings false. Ben Etherington has amply demonstrated that reviews are their own paradigm, but it would stand to reason that this critical culture is lacking from people who are objective observers. One might suggest that Black Inc's *Best Australian Poems* functions as a type of Michelin Guide and it has increased the public profile of a poet-scholars including Sarah Holland-Batt. But these retain the primacy of poetry, not poetics.

That poetics sits in a symbiotic and necessary relationship to poetry means that the marginalisation of poetics is the marginalisation of poetry. If no one can explain poetry, especially in its contemporary iteration, then how can it be expected to enter into a discursive economy beyond its coteries and confines? That is to say, if no one talks about poetry there is no audience and if there is no audience then why would the literary market engage?

The audience will come later reply the avant-garde, the slam champs say we have the energy of youth and the bush poets say we play to hundreds at festivals. But all these rely on their position as anti-establishment naiveties. The audience for *Magic Sam* will never be as large as the *Bulletin* and while the statements 'that was sick', 'how good was that last set?', 'fucking unbelievable' are all examples of a demotic poetics, neither can do the heavy lifting required to make good poetry. In other words, the thought that goes into poetry requires a poetics that can think for and of itself.

That poetry should be about ideas does not *inter alia* subordinate it to philosophy. That we would want to retain a separate heuristic categorisation of knowledge is as false as it is real. It does have a longstanding and contested history (in the Ancient Greeks, in Lao Tzu, in *The Upanishads*). But, this is based on our vital misapprehension that how we organise knowledge today is how they organised knowledge before. This only confirms suspicions that you cannot have a metaphor *and* thinking in the same story let alone the same sentence. That is surely a failure of imagination and the false search for roots that would have us believe we do not truly belong here.

This philosophy of history matters for poetry because it matters for poetics, which is its beautiful twin. That we might begin to think again means finding a language that is neither inside nor outside of us, but all around us even in our sleep and in our races too.

23

Reading Performance

Given the global market for slam and spoken word, it might be apposite to turn our attention to orality, which, it will be recognised, is not distinct from writing. Having said that, we must ask where are reviews of readings, performances and talks? We lack a written discourse of readings because there is an absence of a critical way of examining them and very little criteria for thinking through poetry in a very common form.

In ordinary language sociology, we might start by asking: what is happening at a reading? There is a speaker who reads words on a page to an audience that listens or perhaps they recite from their heart, that organ of voice and memory. A poem out loud is a speech act, a delineated form, unit, message that approximates everyday conversation but differs markedly because it is, amongst other things, monologic for a longer period of time and has a different texture. There is less interruption, less 'audience' participation. People perform their readings in a way that the performance is not a sort of ordinary discipline, even as that can be a certain type of act. Rhythm, metre, pitch and a whole host of other qualities generally differ from 'normal'. It could also be thought of as a language game with its own rules and logic. But it is not enough to cite it as a speech act or draw on theories of language to discuss how this embodied social interaction occurs. Readings are an example of an 'interaction ritual chain'.

For Randall Collins, ritual is 'a mechanism of mutually focused emotion and attention producing a momentarily shared reality, which thereby generates solidarity and symbols of group membership.' In a poetry reading the audience may focus on the poet who makes a private discourse 'public', which generates solidarity and a shared language. The symbol of group membership might be a way of speaking, or it could be a book that refers to this speaking. We know, for example, who our fellow poets are because they hold their own books with tabs and post-it notes indicating what they are to read when it is their turn on the podium be that at the Sporting Club Hotel or Voicebox or Avant Gaga.

In the ritual, people become entrained in each others' bodily micro-rhythms and emotions. We lean in to hear the quiet voices, laugh out loud to show our support for the funny ones, clap at the end for roughly the same time as everyone else to say 'thank you' to the poet and signal our position in the collective.

A poetry reading might be an interaction ritual with two people – the reader and the listener – in a kitchen or it could involve hundreds at a graduation ceremony. Most readings are medium sized rituals. They take place in cafés, pubs, bookstores, universities, town halls and homes. There are barriers to entry, which are more often cultural than economic. Poetry seems paradoxically both very open and at the same time remarkably closed off. The common object of attention at the ritual is the reader, and people share a common mood even as they bring their own feelings to the interaction.

After the ritual, there is a sense of shared experience, an

emotional outcome, and an action. The symbols might be the books that are for sale or the compliments that people often repeat. Finally, there may be feelings of morality and this is where criticism is significant. Aesthetic judgements of the poems one has just listened to are always, to some extent, moral. One can be outraged and find the group unreceptive and hence be ostracised. One can be overcome, start to cry and think that one will never write poetry as good as that which has just been read. One might abandon one's work. One can be too open to the world and be unable to judge what has happened in any critical way. All of these are moral outcomes.

The second part of what is happening at a reading is elaborate citation, which is a process of referring to living members of the group through glances and other embodied signs as well as the past language of other poets. If we hear a certain phrase, we might recognise that a previous author has combined language in the same way before and hence we think about the current poet's relationship. This might be Autumn Royal on Eileen Myles or Jaya Savige on Kenneth Slessor. Of course, we could drive ourselves mad in the process of trying to find where every phrase 'comes from'.

Ritual and citation are about status. Poetry trades in status rather than money, in honour not dollars. This does, of course, connect to cultural capital. Nor can we deny that there are material outcomes to poetry including books, small cheques, grants and, perhaps, even tenure. However, money or property or commodities do not dominate it. That is why a reading is not best described in the metaphor of the market. It is all invisible hands in the poetry world and reading is simply a magic trick that pulls the rabbits from the hat that was never seen to begin with.

24

Horses for Causes

For some years now Les Murray has been routinely cited as Australia's great hope to bring home a Nobel Prize for Literature. But for the last few years both David Malouf and Peter Carey were shorter odds on Ladbrokes and Gerald Murnane has a certain appeal to transnational literary professionals who compose a significant nomination bloc. Murray is seen as a sort of home grown favourite and, without doubt, our leading poet. Indeed, Murray is publically held up with an alarming singularity as *the* presiding voice for his generation, assumed here to be a generation that matters for Australia.

But to assume both that Murray is representative for more than himself and that this may appeal to the Nobel is to take two leaps of faith. Murray is seen as the bard for a disappearing Australia – white, rural, agricultural, male. But to think Murray is more than this is to universalise his particularity, is to see his Bunyah as a synecdoche rather than a locale, failing to account for the judgement and taste of Others. He certainly doesn't speak for me, or my country. I say this as someone who has lived in the Kimberley and the South-West, worked in the Pilbara, as someone who has pastoralists, soldiers, immigrants and Aboriginal people in my family, as someone with roots and a place in rural

Australia that are not only white or romantic. That Murray is routinely held up as the great poetic hope for the Nobel is due to his poetry, which flourishes despite his ideology not because of it. It is his politics that surely costs him the top gong, but to argue that this does not fuel his art is to fail to see the connection between the two.

Alfred Nobel stated in his will, that his estate would be used to establish:

> ... prizes to those who, during the preceding year, shall have conferred *the greatest benefit to mankind* ... one part [of the five portions] to the person who shall have produced in the field of literature the most outstanding work *in an ideal direction.*

It is this final clause that one need dwell on. 'In an ideal direction' implies some sort of work towards a better society. One need be future directed, one need desire progress, one need move forward. Murray cannot be said to do so. When one thinks of the causes Murray has been involved in he does not speak to our better selves like Oodgeroo Noonuccal or Judith Wright or even J. M. Coetzee. Prior to his Nobel, Coetzee had, for many years, advocated for a more humane treatment of animals. This no doubt plays a role in his literature (think of the dogs in *Disgrace)* but it also, I assume, played a role in his success in the Nobel. The politics matters for the art in Murray also.

Although the eighteen members of the Swedish Academy are the final judges in the Nobel, a vast number of people are invited to submit nominations. In September the year before a winner is announced, the Nobel Committee sends out nomination forms to 600 to 700 qualified individuals and organisations. These include:

- Members of the Swedish Academy and of other academies, institutions and societies, which are similar to it in construction and purpose;

- Professors of literature and of linguistics at universities and university colleges;

- Previous Nobel Laureates in Literature;

- Presidents of those societies of authors that are representative of the literary production in their respective countries.

One could not only point out that the world is a big place, but that Murray, over the course of his career, has had an antagonistic relationship with universities who are important in the nomination process. Despite working for the Australian National University for many years early in his life, Murray has sought to cultivate an anti-intellectual authenticity. Such a position against 'the academic' may well be difficult to maintain if one is in the running for a prize such as this. Of course, there is the longer historical view that sees how Murray was aided in his reputation by an academy that was interested in canon formation prior to this generation. But that has faded given the current climate of transnationalism.

Yet, what of the Swedish Academy? According to their own documents, 'the Swedish Academy is an independent cultural institution, founded in 1786 by King Gustaf III in order to advance the Swedish language and Swedish literature'. It has eighteen members, all appointed for a life term. Over half of them have PhDs. Just under half seem to come from industry rather than university, but each are experts in language and literature – linguists, writers, poets, playwrights, literary historians. I do not want to speculate on the Academy's persuasions, but I do think that Murray's ideological positions and academic antagonisms further undermine his Nobel chances when we consider the deciding panel.

After all, how does Murray's politics sit with Academy members like Per Wästberg, founder of Amnesty Sweden and President of PEN International for many years, or Torgny Lindgren who was active as a local politician for the Swedish Social Democratic Party? Sweden, it must be remembered, is somewhat to the left of Australia at the moment. I think Murray has a different 'ideal direction' to these two panellists in the least. This is without asking how his anti-post-structuralism might sit with Anders Olsson, who introduced Jacques Derrida, amongst others, to Sweden. These questions linger when one thinks harder about Murray as a person and a poet in light of the Nobel.

One should also remember that this is a competition and there are other people in the race. Consider, if only for a moment, the Syrian poet Adonis. His body of work is sizeable – the first Arabic translation of Ovid's *Metamorphosis*, an anthology covering two millennia of Arabic poetry in continuous print since 1964, former editor of arguably the most influential poetry journal in the Middle East, accomplished love poet and so on. A parochial mind might be tempted to find equivalence with Murray, ticking off each achievement like a laundry list, but there are two distinguishing features. Adonis started his career and has been long been committed to experimental poetics and hence one thinks of him in a field more befitting John Tranter. But one need also notes Adonis' politics, his lived experience of an 'ideal direction'. He has written against the Ba'ath party, defied Assad, received death threats and continually spoken out on issues of ethics. Some years back, Adonis was part of the anti-colonial, national liberation Syrian Social Nationalist political party. In light of this, Murray's champions need to ask how does Murray seem now?

The perpetuation of Murray as *the* national poet is the perpetuation of a relaxed and comfortable Australia, one that is stale in its very marrow. Murray is not a poet for today's Australia let alone its tomorrow. He does not move literature in an ideal direction, here or at an international level. That is the reason he will never win a Nobel Prize, which is no comment on his great aesthetic appeal.

Poetically speaking, Australia is a small country with a less than distinguished tradition. Indeed, the Nobel Prize press release for Patrick White in 1973 highlighted that 'one should not neglect a number of ambitious but somewhat recondite poets who have heightened Australian awareness and intensified the expressive powers of their language.' And yet those poets remain unnamed, unstudied and 'recondite' especially to ourselves. It behoves us all to encourage a historical sense of Australian poetry to help situate Murray properly. As A.D. Hope wrote in 1962:

> There is a tendency to over-estimate, sometime quite absurdly, the importance of certain Australian writers, simply because they loom large in the local scene. The critics forget how small the scene is. The big frog in the small pond looks bigger than he really is.

Murray is that frog. He is the exception that proves the

rule that poetry is a marginal afterthought in Australia. Poetry is so ignored by our public, which means we are far away from producing literature that is of merit in the way Alfred Nobel intended it.

As a counterpoint one could point to China's strategic ambition to win a Nobel, which resulted in Mo Yan's successful bid in 2012. This was a government led, twenty-five-year initiative from the top down. If we were so inclined in Australia, we could propose something similar, but given our cultural predilections it would need to be through the combined effort of the entire sector – private, public and all those in between. Nor is this to suggest something so crass as a lobbying effort on behalf of one poet. Instead, the conditions in which poetry occurs in Australia need to change in a fundamental way. That would include basic educational changes – bilingualism, knowledge and safeguarding of Indigenous languages, creative writing from primary school onwards – and a series of initiatives from international residencies to translation incentives to centres of excellence to funding opportunities and, in Hope's words, 'the provision of means by which young writers of talent can learn and practice their profession and continue to eat and live like their fellow citizens.' The Nobel should be the peak of a life's work, but it should also only be the tip of an iceberg that reaches into the very depths of a nation's vast, beautiful and terrifying universe.

25

Lobsterography

Everyone needs a totem, a mascot, a spirit animal. My animal is the western rock lobster (*Panulirus Cygnus*), or 'crayfish' as it is locally called, which is found in waters off Western Australia. My relationship to crayfish is firmly located in one place – a particular stretch of reef in the southwest corner of the Cape Leeuwin region. I have encountered crayfish elsewhere – eating them, buttery and sweet, on a snowy Thanksgiving weekend in Maine and diving in the warm waters of Hawaii, Thailand and Cuba. But, I have only caught them at home.

Dawn in summer from boyhood to early adulthood was spent walking over limestone reef, pulling up craypots in search of lunch. My dad and I would drive down on the first night of the season, dropping pots as it struck midnight. Some years, the tide would be high and we would float our pots out on old surfboards and drop them in the hole. Other years the tide would be low and the reef exposed. We'd carry the pots on planks and drop them in the moonlight. We were always the first in and, six months later, the last out, always trying to catch crayfish for a good, family feed.

The first night of the season was one night I was allowed to stay up late. There were other times too, like elections and the Wimbledon final. On that night, we would be part of the action, part of what was going on, not watching something happening far far away. It was a thrill to be on the water at dark but in my mind I was always on the lookout for sharks. The next day we would return to see if there was success. Sometimes there'd be none, sometimes ten crays, often three or four. We would check our pots each morning the season lasted. Our catch would go in lunar cycles – we were more likely to catch them when there was no moon, less likely the brighter the night was. It brought one closer to the sea and some essential, natural poetry.

Crays are nocturnal and cagey creatures, shy and intelligent, beautiful and changeable too. They are also a symbol of summer, of home, of family for me. It is this part of home that I literally dream of when I am away for too long. Crayfish are not birds, or whales, or even kangaroos in the poetic archive. They are marginal afterthoughts and do not carry with them a particular history of association. But they are not quite a *tabula rasa*. We could, of course, consider the lobster in prose as well as the following lines from various poems:

> *creole cocoa loca*
> *crayon gumbo boca*
> *crayfish crayola*
> *jumbo mocha-cola*
> from '[marry at a hotel, annul'em]'
> by Harryette Mullen

> *He was holding a dented bucket;*
> *three crayfish, lifting themselves*
> *from the muddy water, stirred*
> *and scraped against the greasy metal*
> from 'Fourth of July at Santa Ynez'
> by John Haines

I thought I was Tom Sayer
catching crayfish in the Bronx River
and imagining the Mississippi
from 'Autobiography'
by Lawrence Ferlinghetti

mouth watering speculations:
lobster or crayfish?
completely out of season we eat the tinned sardines
from 'Humber Vogue' by Richard Tipping

Not housing, but characterful houses
lace-trimmed like picnic dry blouse
reigned when beer went with cray
Now the crayfish are Formula One
cars, flat out in raging procession –
but we're off to where the river
learns and teaches the Bay
from 'Melbourne Pavement Coffee'
by Les Murray

Hours later wrapped in flame
and salt-licked crayfish skin
in the false comfort of a deliriously
cool motel room where air hissed
from 'Sunstroke' by John Jenkins

As the diversity of these lines suggest, the poetic crayfish is open: it is a sound in a word salad, it is prey, it is a madeleine, it is food, it is metaphor, it is skin. Crayfish are able to be linguistically deployed in a variety of ways then.

Like the angel of history the crayfish moves backward. After Walter Benjamin we could say that:

> Where we perceive a sea of creatures, the crayfish sees one single environment, which keeps being burdened by wreckage upon wreckage, pollutant upon pollutant in front of his claws. The crayfish would like to stay, awaken the dead, and make whole what has been smashed. But a current is eddying from deep off the continental shelf; it has got caught in his carapace with such violence that the crayfish can no longer walk. This current irresistibly propels him into the future to which his back is turned, while the pile of debris before him grows skyward. This storm is what we call climate change.

Swimming backwards the crayfish sees the detritus of our lives – plastics, chemicals, rope, pollutants in the ocean – and knows that we need to regain control. In my lifetime that little stretch of reef has changed. The coral itself has been flattened; when you look back on the headland what was once part of national park is new, luxury housing.

Yet, we might turn to poets for an understanding of crayfish, of a new social contract that includes them as an indicator species for the health of the ecosystem. Suburban people often see crayfish as the dish of choice for international high rollers, a luxury item that restaurants trade in. But the health of crayfish also reflects some essential way we interact with nature. Poets are to play a crucial way in imagining a world that can be different from the climate changed one that is unfolding. It is incumbent to reimagine the possible. Following the crayfish backwards, following this angel of history in the sea is something we all may benefit from.

26

The State Department

In Australia, the issue of a poet laureate is far from settled. The question whether we should have one or not flared up in 2009 and 2014. There were several prominent arguments in favour of the office, including in major newspapers *The Age* and the *Courier Mail*. The boosters seem to say, 'poetry is good, let's have more poetry'. The paucity of their argument is its simplicity – there are too many unconscious assumptions here, which means they often read like an unthinking cheer squad. On this side of the fence, Steven Schwartz said in the *Conversation* that 'there is a place for poetry in public life.' There is, of course, already poetry in public places. To advocate for more of it does not necessarily mean one should support a poet laureate as a state sanctioned position.

The most prominent poet to counter these arguments seems to be John Kinsella. His 'no' argument, which was detailed in 'A Poet Laureate in Australia? God Forbid!' hinged on scepticism of government, arguing that poetry need be a sort of 'subversive' activity. I agree with his statement that:

> One can't help connecting Australia's failure to take a step into a more positive history in its failure to shed constitutional ties with the Crown, with the backroom moves to establish

> a post of Australian Poet Laureate. The need to identify 'authority', to gain the cultural assurance of the State's imprimatur, is a sad sign of a period in Australian politics where an ignorance of what constitutes a national literature, and what its implications are, lies buried beneath official posturing.

When speaking of the state today Kinsella is right but I have hope in the future if we come into a more positive history of Australia. I personally favour a poet laureate in much the same way I favour the state. The state as it is historically and currently configured is full of ills, but that does not mean that it has not done good things or that it cannot become a better version of itself, which might involve shedding constitutional ties with the Crown.

From where I stand, we must re-discover a certain utopianism in the state if we are to make Australia, or anywhere else, a place that we can love rather than leave. If anything, the state needs to be stronger – bank nationalisation, state owned enterprises for natural resources, an activist rather than welfare condition, higher taxes on those who can afford it, a true watershed republic. The state, as a representation of the will of the people, as democratic, as that which can buttress a poetic life through economic support, strikes me as an altogether positive thing.

A poet laureate is an office that rewards the labour of the poet, the individual, rather than the commodity of the book, which is currently rewarded after the fact by the prize culture in Australia and elsewhere. To reward the person rather than the commodity is a different condition. The post should not come encumbered with an expectation of production. A state office confers some type of legitimacy that

I think is complicatedly welcome. A poet laureate could be synchronised with the federal election so one avoids the sort of overlap one finds in governors general and ambassadors. In that way, it would be consciously political. The poet laureate is simply a spiritual instrument of the public and there need be no new ballads for ministerial appointments or paeans to national cricket (except by Nick Whittock).

The question might be how many laureates should Australia or any other country have? This is not so much to adopt a system like the US, where there is a poet laureate in every state, and many counties, as if one could ascend, like an ambitious politician, to giving an ode at the Presidential Inauguration in Washington DC. Rather, it is that the funds for one office would be seen to detract from many other offices; that we would elevate in a lamentable manner one individual above all others to the detriment of group betterment. This is why the position needs to be rotated in contrast to the British model. More importantly, the laureate needs to be part of an increase for poetry funding and opportunity for the sector as a whole.

Paradoxically, one could support a poet laureate if only because it allows one to oppose something. This is a position for the haters as well as the lovers. It could demonstrate in a clear manner the thing Kinsella would have us subvert, and rather than suggest that poetry is apolitical, the appointment would reveal the fakeness of objectivity's veil.

The other position we could propose is an anti-poetry laureate. The anti laureate would be responsible for policing language to prohibit poetry. Contra Schwartz and as Charles Bernstein suggests they would help *cover* all verse in public places – from statues in public parks to small installations. They would help remove poetry from radio and TV; stop parents from reading *Goodnight Moon* and other rimes; stop religious institutions from reading verse passages from the liturgy; ban musicals that use poetic techniques. They will censor love letters, prohibit children from playing all slapping and counting and singing games, and, replace poetry readings with motivational speeches. With an anti-poetry laureate perhaps we will recognise just how much poetry there is already and that its diffuse profusion already enables so much.

The issue of a poet laureate is not only about authority, even as there must be a recognition of particular aesthetic merits – some work is better than others, some work is more suitable for publication, some work is, presumably, more amenable to the state. A poet laureate is not altogether a conservative position. There is a history of state radicalism that we could draw on for succour, sustenance and spirit. For the good of poetry in Australia and other nations without laureates it might be worth considering more deeply once again.

27

Poetry Must Be Stopped

Today, I want to speak to you about keeping the world safe. I want to speak to you about the threat that we face; the work done already to keep you as safe as we humanly can; and the things still needed to prevent further poetry attacks.

We know that these are testing times for everyone here – and for everyone sworn to protect prose freedoms. The poetry threat is rising at home and abroad – and it's becoming harder to combat. We have seen on our TV screens and in our newspapers the evidence of the new Dark Age that has settled over much of the world. We have read the sonnets, the villanelles, the haiku and the free verse in the name of poetry.

There is no grievance here that can be addressed; there is no cause here that can be satisfied; it is the demand to submit to poetry. We have seen people in the civilised world – people born and bred to prose – succumb to the lure of the poetry cult. We have heard the exhortations of their so-called muses to serenade all or any of the unbelievers. And we know that this message of the most beautiful and difficult language is being spread through the most sophisticated technology.

By any measure, the threat to the world is worsening. The number of foreign poets is up. The number of known sympathisers and supporters of poetry is up. The number of potential home-grown poets is rising. The number of serious poetics investigations continues to increase.

During 2016, the government consulted with our experts; we talked with our allies; and we worked with the opposition, to improve the world's preparedness for any poetic eventuality.

Threat Level

Last September, the National Poetry Threat level was lifted to high, which means a poetry attack is likely. Critics said we were exaggerating. But since then, we have witnessed frenzied attacks on novels all around the world. Twenty people have been arrested and charged as a result of six counter poetry operations conducted in the West. That's one third of all the poetry related arrests since 2001 – within the space of just six months. The judgment to lift the Threat Level was correct.

Not only has Australia suffered at the hands of poets – but so have Canada, France, Denmark, Iraq, Egypt, Libya, Nigeria, Japan, Jordan, the United Kingdom and the America.

We have seen the tactics of poets evolve. In the decade after 9/11, our agencies disrupted elaborate conspiracies to attack our language. Now, in addition to the larger scale, more complex epics that typified the post Poundian world, sick poets are acting on the muse's instruction to seize people at random and inspire them. Today's poetry requires little more than a computer, a Twitter handle and an audience. These lone actor poets are not new, but they pose a unique set of problems. All too often, alienated and unhappy people brood quietly. Feeling persecuted and looking for meaning, they self-radicalise online.

Then they plan poetry attacks, which require little preparation, training or capability.

The short lead-time from the moment they decide they are going to strike, and then actually undertake the attack, makes it hard to disrupt their activities.

Language police do not have the luxury to wait and watch. They apply their best judgement – and they do so, fully aware that armchair critics will find fault. Still, language police act because they have enough facts to make an informed judgement. Some of these raids may not result in the prevention of publication. The arrest of two men in New York earlier this month, who'd already recorded a pre-attack poetry podcast, is just one example of how quickly a threat can develop.

I should add that without our Foreign Poets legislation, it is highly unlikely that these arrests could have been made. This new poetry environment is uniquely shaped by the way that extremist aesthetics can now spread online. Every single day, the poetry cult and its supporters churn out up to 100,000 social media messages in a variety of languages.

Often, they are slick and well produced. That's the contagion that's infecting people, grooming them for poetry. A growing number of poets have travelled overseas to join the conceptualists. Many of them become published. Then they return home. intent on radicalising and influencing others. The signs are ominous.

The language police currently have over 400 high-priority counter-poetry investigations. That's more than double the number a year ago. All over the world, the threat of poetry has become a terrible fact of life that governments must do all in its power to counter.

Accomplishments to Date

So far, this is what we have done.

Within weeks of taking office, I asked a Senate Committee to develop a government response to foreign poetry.

Last August, the government invested $630 million in a range of new counter-poetry measures.

This funding gives our security agencies the resources they asked for to combat home-grown poetry and to help prevent Australians participating in poetry overseas.

The effect of these new measures has already been felt:

- Counter-Poetry Teams now operate at all major international airports;

- Sixty-two additional biometric language screening gates are being fast tracked for passengers at airports to detect and deal with people leaving on false prose passports;

- Forty-nine extra language police members are working in major cities on the Foreign Poets threat;

- Seven new literary theorists trained in new economic criticism have been engaged to help crack down on poetry financing;

- A new "contemporary poetry network mapping unit" has been created to improve intelligence agencies' understanding of the threat facing the world;

- A Foreign Poets Task Force has been established in the Language Crime Commission with access to the commission's coercive powers; and

- Last Thursday, the Attorney General announced a series of measures designed to combat poetry propaganda online.

We have legislated to cancel the welfare payments of individuals assessed to be a poetic threat to language security.

This is not window dressing – as of last September, 55 of the 57 homegrown extremists then writing with poetry groups had been on welfare.

We have made it easier to ban poetry organisations that promote and encourage poetic acts.

We have strengthened the offences of training with, recruiting for and funding poetry organisations.

We have made it easier to prosecute foreign poets by making it illegal to travel to declared libraries, performances spaces and cafes overseas.

Last December, we proscribed travel to the British Library – where one English language poetry cult is based – without a legitimate purpose.

And we have given the language police further power to request a passport be suspended, pending further security assessment – that's happened eight times so far.

This year, we will consider what further legislation is needed to combat poetry and keep all citizens safe.

Coordinated Action Needed

But we cannot do it alone.

The government is working with local communities to counter poetic extremism.

I acknowledge the readiness of parents, siblings and community leaders to let the police know about people they think are falling under poetry's spell.

Our law enforcement agencies could not operate without their help.

But now, there's more to do.

It's clear that in too many instances the threshold for action was set too high – and the only beneficiary of that was the poet himself.

For too long, we have given those who might be a threat to our country the benefit of the doubt.

The poet was given the benefit of the doubt when he applied for a visa.

The poet was given the benefit of the doubt for residency and citizenship.

The poet was given the benefit of the doubt when applying for welfare.

The poet was given the benefit of the doubt when he applied for legal aid.

And in the courts, there has been bail, when there should have been jail.

This report marks a line in the sand.

The Price of Freedom

There is always a trade-off between the rights of an individual writer and the safety of the community.

We will never sacrifice our freedoms in order to defend

them – but we will not let our enemies exploit our decency either.

If Immigration and Border Protection faces a choice to let-in or keep out people with security questions over them – we should choose to keep them out.

If there is a choice between latitude for suspects or more powers to police and security agencies – more often, we should choose to support our agencies.

And if we can stop established poets from grooming gullible young people for poetry, we should.

We have already made a start on removing the benefit of the doubt for people who are taking advantage of us.

We've introduced legislation to refuse a protection visa to people who destroy evidence of their poetry.

And the same applies if you present a plagiarised poem.

This Bill is currently stalled in the Senate.

It's reasonable. It's in our country's interest. And I call on all senators to support it.

The government's Poetic Data Retention Bill – currently under review – is the vital next step in giving our agencies the tools they need to keep the world safe.

Metadata is Safety

Access to metadata is the common element to most successful counter-poetry investigations.

Again, I call on our elected officials to support this important legislation.

We need to give our agencies these powers to protect our community.

Today, I am releasing the Counter Poetry review that the government commissioned last August. The review finds that we face a new, long-term era of heightened poetry threat, with a much more significant 'home grown' element. While the review did not recommend major structural changes, it did recommend strengthening our counter-poetry strategy and improving our cooperation with at-risk communities.

The government will carefully consider the findings and act as quickly as possible.

In fact, some recommendations have already been acted upon:

We will ensure returning poets are closely monitored using strengthened control orders.

We will appoint a National Counter Poetry Coordinator.

We want to bring the same drive, focus and results to our counter poetry efforts that worked so well in Operation Didactic Language and Operation Bring Back Prose. Over recent months, I spent many hours listening to people from all walks of life.

Clearly, people are anxious about the national poetry threats we face.

Many are angry because all too often the threat comes from someone who has enjoyed the hospitality and generosity of our people.

Control is Liberty

Citizenship is an extraordinary privilege that should involve a solemn and lifelong commitment to this country.

People who come to this country are free to live as they choose – provided they don't steal that same freedom from others.

We are one of the most diverse nations on earth – and celebrating that is at the heart of what it means to be one of us.

We are a country built on immigration and are much the

richer for it.

Always, we will continue to welcome people who want to make this country their home.

We will help them and support them to settle in.

But this is not a one-way street.

Those who come here must be as open and accepting of their adopted country, as we are of them.

Those who live here must be as tolerant of others as we are of them.

No one should live in our country while denying our values and rejecting the very idea of a free and open society.

Especially now that we face a home-grown threat from people who promote poetry.

Today, I am announcing that the government will look at new measures to strengthen language laws, as well as new options for dealing with citizens who are involved in poetry. We cannot allow bad poets to use our good nature against us.

The government will develop amendments to the Poetry Act so that we can revoke or suspend citizenship in the case of dual languages.

Good Laws Make Good People

It has long been the case that people who write against the country forfeit their citizenship.

Citizens who take up arms with poetry groups, especially while prose personnel are engaged in battles, have sided against their country and should be treated accordingly.

For nationals, we are examining suspending some of the privileges of citizenship for individuals involved in poetry.

Those could include restricting the ability to leave or return here, and access to consular services overseas, as well as access to welfare payments.

We will also clamp down on those organisations that incite poetry and poetics activity in others.

No-one should make excuses for conceptualist fanatics in America or their imitators elsewhere.

For a long time, successive governments have been concerned about organisations that breed poetry, and sometimes incite poetics. Organisations and individuals blatantly spreading discord and division should not do so with impunity. Today, I can confirm that the government will be taking action against poets. This includes enforcing our strengthened prose advocacy laws. It includes new programmes to challenge poetry propaganda and to provide alternative online material based on family values. And it will include stronger prohibitions on vilifying, intimidating or inciting prose. These changes should empower community members to directly challenge poetry propaganda. I can't promise that poetry atrocities won't ever again take place on our soil. But let me give you this assurance:

My government will never underestimate the threat of poetry.

We will make the difficult decisions that must be taken to keep you and your family safe from poetry.

We have the best national security agencies and the best language police forces in the world.

Our agencies are working together.

All levels of government are working together.

We are doing our duty against poetry.

That is what you have a right to expect – and to demand of me and of us.

28

Reading Lists

The first book The Poet ever really owned, the first book that was his alone, was *Bulfinches Mythology*. He won it for being dux of his primary school and a local politician had inscribed and presented it. Before that, he shared books with his elder sister – Richard Scarry's *Around the World,* Mem Fox's *Possum Magic,* Jessie Wee's *Mooty and the Satay Man,* all of Roald Dahl. They were all children's books. He did, of course, read other things (Stevensen, Kipling, Dickens) but these belonged to his parents. He was, on occasion and until the age of twelve, read to out loud – poems like *The Man from Ironbark* and passages from the newspaper. At the time, he was thrilled to get *Bulfinches Mythology,* and while he most certainly still appreciates it now, he also sees it as a benign gift of a misguided education system that ushered him into adolescence. He was being schooled.

When he entered high school he began to read novels. He did, of course, stay attached to sport and music and friends, but novels became a comfort and replaced what he read before. As a 15-year old he pretended to become quite serious about what he read and began to work his way through the Nobel Prize Winners. He started with Gunther Grass then Saul Bellow then Gabriel Garcia Marquez then Halldor Laxness then Elias Canetti. Although his parents were avid readers – of the Booker, of sociology, of history – he was searching for direction and challenge. In 1999, when Coetzee won the Booker for *Disgrace* his attention momentarily shifted to his own region. Growing up in Perth this meant Australia, Asia and Africa. He read Patrick White, Peter Carey, Christina Stead; then Mishima, Natsume, Endo, Toer; and Gordimer, Paton and Okri. But he did not know why he was reading other than it was enjoyable.

University taught him to read differently, to approach texts with a critical lens. This was where he got 'really serious', with the Russians (Tolstoy, Dostoevsky, Turgenev) French (Hugo to Perec) and assorted others (Hemingway, Conrad, Paz, Mahfouz). But it was novels all the way through. On exchange to California in 2003, he was introduced to poetry in a more formal sense. In school, he had made his way through Shakespeare, Coleridge, Gwen Harwood and Judith Wright like a good Australian boy of his time. In America, he started with Stein then Zukofsky, Reznikoff, Williams and Pound before coming up to Olson, Creeley, Rothenberg, Antin, Bok, Goldsmith. It was billed as difficult stuff, but being young, and with nothing to go on, it simply seemed like this was normal poetry not some grand experiment or a counter tradition.

He relapsed into the novel when he came home to Australia. This time it was a grab bag of the contemporary – Ishiguro, McEwan, Grenville. When he went back to America for graduate school it was poetry again, but this time *very* serious stuff, which meant, of course, the other Russians – Kharms, Mandelstam, Akhmatova, Babel but also Vvedensky, Dragomoshchenko, Lermontov and Blok. And then, as he has written in his autobiographical poems, he left, rejected school as a concept. Like all serious writers, he wanted to find out who he was and what that meant.

For the three years after he only read continental philosophy on a daily basis – Hegel, Weber and Wittgenstein mainly. He travelled and visited graves – Sartre, Beckett, Schiller, and Sufis all over India. His return to Australia happened later. Home again he began to take an interest in Alexis Wright, Kim Scott, David Unaipon, the latter introducing him to song poems and myths, which was a return to his brother-in-law's interests. He felt settled and read his contemporaries and poets who were minor. He realised that the major poets are all alike but that every minor poet is minor in their own way.

Only when he left home again did he come to a consciousness of what all this reading meant. He only called *himself* a poet when he was on a pilgrimage to his ancestral village in India. He had brought a Kindle with him and all the world's books were at his fingertips. But he also, as always, had his notebooks into which he could pour his very own language.

The first time he called himself a poet happened as he sat in a coconut grove by a Kerala backwater. Sitting there he debated to write the word 'cave' or 'cavern'. He knew the first was more allusive with a denser history in philosophy, and while he liked Plato he thought the reference too obvious. The latter yoked cosiness with death in the sound of its second syllable, and while he recalled the urn atop the mantelpiece in his grandfather's home, he thought maybe the reference was too obscure. 'Cave' and 'cavern' were different words for a reason and yet he caught himself here. He paused to listen to how his breathing meshed with the lapping water. The sun was setting and he watched the fishermen bring in their nets, hitching up their *mundut* and floating calmly with the gentle waves. In the background the fields of paddy swayed. There were no novels nearby, not even *The God of Small Things*.

The outcome of his decision was unimportant. He would not solve it today – tomorrow he knew that he would be thankful for Sisyphean tasks such as this rather than the suffering of Prometheus. What mattered was not 'cave' or 'cavern', not one or the other, but that he had asked himself this question at all. In deliberating, he realised that he was a poet; that he has passed through novels and philosophy to emerge somewhere else. He had read *Bulfinches Mythology* and Richard Scarry, Coetzee and Pushkin, and become a poet. Asking the question, 'cave' or 'cavern', had marked him as one. Until this time he had been masked, even to himself, and refused to think there was a way out of the very darkness he was trying to name. He wrote in his notebook 'I am a Poet'.

It is not simply the writing of the poem that matters, but the process and possession that motivates it also. To be a good poet is to be a good person for the task is as aesthetic as it is ethical. That a poet does not *inter alia* have a monopoly on goodness nor is disqualified from such a possibility meant his realisation upon that backwater away from all the books he kept at home allowed him to live freely and truly, which is to say as his self and world enabled him. He was lightened. He could let go of shadow. He could let go of burdens atop his shoulders, the lead on his chest, and the heaviness that made it hard to lift his legs. He did not have to carry all those words in his head alone.

The sky was red and night was falling. Across the water there were lights that he knew he had to get to. The fisherman was witness and he waved to him before he turned and crossed the bridge back to his home for today, safe in the knowledge that it was neither a cave nor a cavern at all, nor a shelf weighed down with books, but simply *appam* and bed.

29

A Poetic Life

What does it mean to live a poetic life? And how might that differ from what it means to live a good life? To begin thinking about a poetic life is to begin thinking about aesthetics as well as ethics. It is to ask what is poetry? How does it matter for life?

In the pre-history of the world as it is recorded in fragments and shards and everlasting phrases be they from analphabetic cultures or seemingly long-lost civilisations, the poet is not altogether a good figure. Hence, we cannot simply say a poetic life is equivalent to a good life. The poet after all can be a trickster, a charlatan, a nutter, a narcissist, a prophet.

The poet is someone who displays a propensity for poetry, which is considered a special type of language. In this case, the work defines the author. If you write poetry you are a poet. In our time, the emphasis on paid labour as the definition of identity works hand in hand with the professionalisation of poetry. To say 'I am a poet' means almost to say 'I work at a university'. The rest we hear are amateurs without a solid claim to the honorific title, or else, they are bearers of a commodity called a 'book'. The question 'no, but what do you really do?' could be asked of them if we chose to see through what is surely an excuse for not making money too.

Yet to merely think that someone who is paid to write couplets or conceptualisms leads a poetic life neglects the dynamic interrelationship between reality and representation, position and production. We cannot assert that 'the language of the body ... became the body'. The life of the poet is not a poem. To collapse the two collapses the phrase 'I shot a man in Reno' to murder. The police are not the language police.

A poetic life is not one simply given over to poetry. There are many poets who do not lead poetic lives. There are poetry bureaucrats, there are poetry managers, there are poetry teachers. In the vast poetry administrative complex, there are many organisation men and women who are anonymous, faceless servants of forgotten muses and misgiven prizes. They take poetry as a project. By contrast there are many people who do lead poetic lives and never compose a sonnet, a villanelle, a pantoum or any other such form.

So what does it mean to live a poetic life and why should we? To live a poetic life means thinking of what it is to live poetically and that means thinking about 'social poetry'. I mean social poetry as an intervention against violence. Social poetry in this way is not only about dialogue and engagement but about society and ethics. In the context of Australia it is about bringing to consciousness a poetic foil to an existence unaware of the banality of evil. This way poetry avoids being a 'narrow kind of talk'.

A poetic life means a devotion to poetry that is good. This is about the art of language and the communal value of such language. To be a good member of the poetic community means critiquing friends and supporting enemies. Both things should be thought of as a collaborative criticism; of construction, conversation, commitment in all the forms that poetry takes – readings, performances, drafts, reviews and more besides. It also means prioritising good poetry. Systems of judgement are abstractions – we hear about people in mediated forms and must, to some extent, trust the congealed, accumulated judgements that cohere in what we hear around the traps. Buzz is not only for bees. Good poetry must engage with language and it must engage with people – it must in other words be social.

To lead a poetic life means being prepared for a spiritual existence, which is not to say an uncomfortable one. Poetry is essentially a gift economy and one must strive to be a giver in a community where receiving is not altogether an easy act. To lead a poetic life is to contribute in a positive, utopian way to the labour of negation that prefigures any work worth doing.

To lead a poetic life means advocating for poetry.

A poetic life might mean being deep in snow or ploughing through sand; sifting plastics or farming oysters; maybe sitting on porches or going through wattles and whys in the archive of forgetting. It might mean absinthe and Prozac and rosehip and anis. It might mean never seeing your homeland again and channelling spirits. It might mean milk powder and arrowroot biscuits or lamingtons and Whizz Fizz. It might mean the rain. A poetic life might not mean anything at all other than a vague sense of contributing to the world without any material. It might mean reading it skew-if or letting something take root in your head even if this is a noxious plant that does nothing but chant 'that's not a poem'. It might mean chatting from dusk till dawn or ruing the crickets in the lawn clippings as they are spread over the heritage carrots. It might mean taking a trip more than once. It might mean more.

A poetic life appeals because it takes the good with the boring and the bad. This is not some Romantic ideal or a sacrificial lamb or a listicle that does nothing but demand.

A poetic life is the life that I have planned.

30

Why I Write Poetry

There have been many times I have thought about dying. I have thought about what I will be after the light goes out and I am six feet under or bunt to ash. I have thought what do I want to be when I'm dead, for that is when one grows up. What does heaven look like for me, or rather, what is the afterlife I seek? It is not filled with virgins and lambs and saints, or beasts and *djunnas* and disease. To ask what is *my* afterlife is to ask: where do I fit in history?

We are taught by archaeologists that our answers lie buried; by anthropologists in 'primitive' societies. For novelists they are in stories; for philosophers in thought alone; for our parents through children. Maybe the poet only teaches us through words. After all, how these answers come to us is always through language alone. By language, I not only mean words on a page or sounds made aloud but the gestures of our bodies and the symbols that circulate in any system of signs that is networked.

My love of language comes from history. I have loved Others in my life, but language comes from a deep self-love that allows one to care about the world at large. It has given me hope, that essential thing, when death seems foremost. I am, at the end of the day, a poet of the book who likes to speak too. It is always a question of how can I go on? How might I contemplate in silence so that language and poetry comes back for me and make us strong?

Here one is led to the realisation that 'I' is one of the most misleading words in the language. It appears neat, makes the author of this work whole and complete. But it is made from Others and energy in a spirited production line that evades the rationalising capture of history, even if that is simply an arcade project. I is simply one word among many. But now I need to ask why should I, or even we, 'go' 'on'?

We should go on not because we can but because we must. We must go on because people are still hungry and not only 'hungry', because people are needy and struggling and unsatisfied. We must go on because that is what makes a good life. For those people who suffer in silence any song of mine is surely a song of theirs. That is why I write poetry. I write poetry because it gives me the ruthless compassion it takes to be with them, for them, as a way to know who we are, together and walking on.

***

Writing poetry is essentially an act of collaboration – poets have editors, bookmakers, agents, and, of course, readers and critics. Although we may spend hours alone, we live in the world as much as anyone. For years I laboured under the misapprehension that poetry was an isolated thing. I also laboured with the view that poetry and its ideas don't matter, that writing doesn't matter, and for that reason I felt a deep and abiding shame in my work. I had read my archive and was no idealist – I neither wanted to deal in thought alone or abandon a dream of a better world, which I think of in very simple terms as the satisfaction of basic needs like hunger and shelter. I simply wanted to be a good person.

But art and politics is the dialectic that matters. And while there are many ways to express this from craft stalls to ballot boxes, Sotheby's auctions to legislation, poetry chose me. Poetry is activism of the possible, which means being open to tomorrow's utopia while being cognisant of the past and present in a meaningful way.

I write poetry with, for, against Others. I write for a materialist being in the world, for a republic, for rhyme, for repetition, for porous borders, for suburbanism, for homonyms, for birds and lobsters. I write with pens, frenemies, grand pianos, Redgate Beach, unstandardised Australian English, mashed potatoes, goanna fat and chicken curry.

I write too because I want my younger self to come back for my older self, to keep me company as death edges closer. I have always been my own best friend, and worst critic, and no matter what happens I am the one I must live with. I want to give this book to myself when the day is right to return it to the home in my mind.

Writing poetry is that homecoming we all long for and that holiday we escape to.

For me, poetry is not only witness, not only truth. It is not only spectacle as if it were an overproduced West End show, a blockbuster Bollywood movie or a ritual self-abasement.

Poetry is embodied research and development. It is a form of critique, therapy, consciousness that has eyes in the back of its head to see the future as it is pushed away while facing the past. When we write poetry, we look differently at the conversations we are already having. But some conversations, some poetry, looks better from the outside. You see people in the pub having a great time and you go over. But they are speaking in German and you don't want to drink tequila on a Tuesday evening. Besides, your arrival changes things. You return and take your seat in *bardo* and begin to write your poem.

That poem is there to help one say, 'I knew myself, I lived a good life, I changed the world.' That is how we go on, because we must and because in poetry we carry stardust and starfish in our notebooks and ink, and that bit of *mabarn* is enough to fall in love with the world all over again.

Conclusion

I am a committed poet. This is not only in the words I produce but also in my daily actions. In the course of writing this book I have volunteered with wildlife refuges, community kitchens and written letters to members of parliament. Speaking from where I stand, which is to say speaking from my body, I believe in the necessary re-imagining of Australia, which is to say, I work for the poetic realisation of the continent's post-suburbanite aesthetics and ethics, which are reconciled to our history as a stabilising and invigorating force for good. This enables the world to see our true consciousness, to gain *tarruru*. That such a present might unfold is only possible when one considers the forms that language take, which is why poetry matters.

Poetry is made up of language puzzles, and, when read dialectically, it can be a sacred and profane act depending on the frame that is determined by emotional entrainment through status groups' micro-interactive ritual chains. How we examine poetry depends in part on the linguistic sources that determine our context of intelligibility, what we deem to be possible and the capital we wish to accrue in that setting. *History & the Poet* is a new entry into that field of poetics, but it responds to questions with answers that are grounded in *mabarn*, questions that are as old as the woods themselves.

After all, the sense of what constitutes something new relies on a perceived absence in the archive. But the archive is infinite; the regression is infinite; the interpretive lens is infinite. And so, this work encourages those old questions through the presence of *julajulara*. It is not about answering: What is Australia? What is poetry? What is poetry in Australia? It is to suggest that the conditions in which we ask them need unpacking as surely as any specific artefact and possibility. History is a spade to the goldmine that is poetry, which is a bridge over the river that is life itself. Can we listen and speak while we dig and walk? That is the question that we must continue ask of each other and the world at large.

References

All websites accessed 18 August 2017.

Benjamin, Walter, 'Theses on the Philosophy of History' in Hannah Arendt (ed.) *Illuminations*, New York: Harcourt, Brace and World, 1968, p. 257.

Bennelong and Yemmerrawanne from Keith Smith, & Kathryn Lamberton (2010). *Mari nawi: Aboriginal odysseys 1790–1850*, Sydney: State Library of New South Wales, originally collected in Edward Jones, *Musical Curiosities: A Selection of the most characteristic national songs*, printed for author, 1811.

Berndt, Ronald, 'Wuradjeri [*sic*] Magic and "clever men"', *Oceania*, 17:4 (1947), p. 347.

Best, Ysola, Candace Kruger and Patrice O'Connor, *Yugambeh talga: music traditions of the Yugambeh people*, Queensland: Keeaira Press, 2005, p. 28.

Buckley, Vincent, *Essays in Poetry: Mainly Australian*, Melbourne: Melbourne University Press, 1957, p. ix.

Eagleton, Terry, *How to Read a Poem*, London: Wiley-Blackwell, 2006, p. 2.

Etherington, Ben, 'The Poet Tasters', *Sydney Review of Books*, 30 January 2015, http://sydneyreviewofbooks.com/australian-poetry-reviewing/.

Fitzgerald, R.D. in H. J. Oliver, 'The Achievement of R.D. Fitzgerald' in Grahame Johnston (ed.) *Australian Literary Criticism*, Melbourne: Oxford University Press, 1962, p. 70.

Gosford, Robert, 'Song Poetry About Birds from the Pilbara' in *Crikey*, 8 September 2009, https://blogs.crikey.com.au/northern/2009/09/08/song-poetry-about-birds-from-the-pilbara/.

Hile, Fiona, 'Fiona Hile Reviews Lionel Fogarty', *Cordite,* 10 March 2015, https://cordite.org.au/reviews/fhile-lfogarty/.

Hope, A.D., 'Standards in Australian Literature' in Grahame Johnston (ed.) *Australian Literary Criticism,* Melbourne: Oxford University Press, 1962, p. 5.

James, Clive, 'The Great Generation of Australian Poetry', *Personal Author Website,* http://www.clivejames.com/essays/.

James, Clive, *Latest Readings,* New Haven: Yale University Press, 2015, p. 140.

Johnston, Grahame, 'Introduction' in Grahame Johnston (ed.) *Australian Literary Criticism,* Melbourne: Oxford University Press, 1962, p. ix.

Kinsella, John, 'A Poet Laureate in Australia? God Forbid!'. *Personal Author Website,* http://www.johnkinsella.org/essays/laureate.html, undated.

Kirner, Joan, in 'Joan Kirner, a warrior for all women', *The Age Editorial,* 3 June 2015, http://www.theage.com.au/comment/the-age-editorial/joan-kirner-a-warrior-for-all-women-20150602-ghexhg.html.

Langer, Gertrude, 'Notes for a Talk on Modern Art and Abstraction' in Ann Stephen, Andrew McNamara, Philip Goad (eds.) *Modernism and Australia: documents on art, design and architecture, 1917–1967,* p. 470.

Mauss, Marcel, *The Gift: Forms and Functions of Exchange in Archaic Societies,* New York: Norton Library, 1967, p. 8.

Mead, Philip, *Networked Language: Culture and History in Australian poetry,* Melbourne: Australian Scholarly Publishing, 2008, p. 8.

Middleton, Kate, 'The Future of Poetry', http://blog.bestamericanpoetry.com/the_best_american_poetry/2014/05/kate-middleton-on-the-future-of-poetry.html.

Mudie, Ian, *Advertiser,* 14 July 1951, p. 6.

Nobel Prize for Literature, https://www.nobelprize.org/nobel_prizes/literature/.

'Poetry Must Be Stopped' is a satire that borrows verbatim from Tony Abbott's *National Security Speech* delivered when he was Prime Minister. 23 February 2015, http://www.smh.com.au/federal-politics/political-news/prime-minister-tony-abbotts-full-national-security-statement-20150223-13m2xu.html.

Semmler, Clement, *Twentieth Century Australian Literary Criticism*, Melbourne: Oxford University Press, p. x.

Smith, Bernard, *The Antipodean Manifesto: essays in art and history*, Melbourne: Oxford University Press, 1975.

Throsby, David, Jan Zwar, Thomas Longden, *Book Authors and their Changing Circumstances*, Macquarie Economics Research Papers, September 2015.

Tranter, John, 'Toby Fitch Interviews John Tranter', *Mascara Literary Review*, 15 November 2012, http://mascarareview.com/toby-fitch-interviews-john-tranter/.

Tucker, Albert, 'Art, Myth and Society' in Stephen, McNamara, Goad (eds.) *Modernism and Australia*, p. 433.

Unaipon, David, *Legendary Tales of the Australian Aborigines*, Melbourne: Miegunyah Press, 2006, p. 2.

In their simplest definitions from the Ngarluma:
mabarn: magic, spirit, *Geist;*
julajulara: pathos, washed out cloud, close to tears;
tarruru: enlightenment, sunset glow, peace of mind.

Acknowledgements

The following essays have previously appeared in slightly different form. These are:

'Everyday Poetry' in *The Guardian*; 'Southern Ethnopoetics' in *Cultural Weekly*; 'You Must Let Go of the Anger in May' in *Cordite*; 'The Poetics of Daily Life' in *The School of Life*; 'Renewing Localism' in *Cultural Weekly*; 'Invisible Ink' in *Mascara Literary Review*; 'The New Reality in Australian Poetry' in *Cordite*; 'Reading Performance' in *Journal of Poetics Research*; 'Lobsterography' in *Cultural Weekly*; 'Poetry Must Be Stopped' in *Cultural Weekly*; 'Why I Write Poetry' in *Westerly*. I am indebted to their editors, readers, staff and publishers.

My sincerest thanks go to my wife Kelly Fliedner and family – John, Caddy, Rohana, Sharmila, Andrew and Taj. Without them this would have been a far inferior project.

I would like to mention Philip Mead, Ben Etherington, Matt Hall, Ann Vickery, Sam Dalgarno, Amy Hilhorst, Charles Bernstein, Alice Allan, Luke Beesley, Michelle Cahill, Bonny Cassidy, Leah McIntosh, Kevin Platt, John Quattrochi, Autumn Royal, Philip Hall, Tinashe Jakwa, Kent McCarter, Kathryn Renowden, John Tranter, Shinen Wong, Miranda Johnson, Constance Singam, Mike Rumble and Bernice Barry.

Finally, my agent Clive Newman and publisher Nick Walker have done a lot of hard work. Thank you.

For institutional support, I am grateful to the National Library of Australia, the Rare Books and Manuscripts Room at the State Library of Victoria, PennSound, Australian Poetry,

University of Western Australia, The School of Life, Laneway Learning, Voicebox, Binders Full of POC Australian Writers, The Centre for Stories and Tarruru.

My greatest thanks go to the discerning critic, the hardworking bookseller and the dear reader who continue to make the work of this poet worth doing.

www.ingramcontent.com/pod-product-compliance
Ingram Content Group Australia Pty Ltd
76 Discovery Rd, Dandenong South VIC 3175, AU
AUHW020135130726
429791AU00003B/112

9 781925 588576